S0-AAD-185

Cover Art by Elna Rydzewski

CATERFLY

by Don De Paul

A QUEST BOOK

*This publication made possible
with the assistance of the Kern Foundation*

THE THEOSOPHICAL PUBLISHING HOUSE

Wheaton, Ill., U.S.A. / Madras, India / London, England

©Copyright 1977 by Don DePaul
All rights reserved

A Quest original, published by the Theosophical
Publishing House, a department of The
Theosophical Society in America. Inquiries for
permission to reproduce all, or portions of this
book, should be addressed to Quest Books,
306 West Geneva Road, Wheaton, Illinois 60187.

A Quest original,
published by the
Theosophical Publishing House,
a department of
The Theosophical Society in America.
Inquiries for permission
to reproduce all, or portions of
this book, should be addressed to
Quest Books,
306 West Geneva Road,
Wheaton,   Illinois   60187.

Library of Congress Catalog Number: 76-39691
ISBN: 0-8356-0490-X

Printed in the United States of America

DEDICATION

This book is dedicated to
my beloved wife, Tonia,
whose faith in life inspired the
writing of this story;
to Marc and Kim, our Caterflies;
and to our remarkable mothers,
Claire and Teddi;
it is for all those who quest
for meaning in life.
With deep appreciation for
John P., our teacher,
and the little brown bee who
taught him, and all those
who point out a Way to us.

CONTENTS

Chapter 1

. . . in which Caterfly is led to believe he's a butterfly.

Caterfly sat on the middle of the lowest branch of the cherry tree and sobbed softly.

Except for the unhappiness of the blue and white striped insect, the little garden seemed peaceful and happy. Every insect, bird, fish, and animal followed its instincts or some inner plan and carried out its mission in life with the minimum of self-pity or sorrow.

Caterfly felt he could never find peace or happiness in this lovely garden or anywhere, for that matter, because he was different.

"All robins look like robins," he thought, "and all the goldfish in the little pond below at least look like fish. All caterpillars resemble caterpillars and certainly all butterflies look like butterflies, but I look like nothing—nothing at all. I must be nothing!"

While he was in the midst of his daily depression, he felt a soft nudge on the tip of his tail. It was Homer, a bright green caterpillar who had been very helpful to him since he had emerged from his cocoon three months before. Homer had sensed that Caterfly had special problems from the very beginning of their friendship. He constantly protected his strange-looking friend from the vicious mockery of the other caterpillars who called Caterfly "freak," "weirdo," or "show off." A few caterpillars thought the strange one was an agent sent by the butterflies to spy upon them for some unknown reason.

"Down again, old pal?" Homer said cheerfully as he crawled alongside Caterfly and turned to face him antenna to antenna.

"Yes, I'm sorry I'm such a bore, but. . ."

"But-you-don't-know-what-you-are!" interrupted Homer.

"Yes, that's right, Homer."

"I told you what you are, Caterfly. You are not one of us."

"How can I be just not something or just not some group or just a non-you? I am unhappy because I don't know what I am. Everyone else is happy because they know what they are."

"Caterfly, would it make you happy if I told you that you are a caterpillar with wings?"

"A freak, you mean?"

"Well different. The world is caterpillars and non-caterpillars. That's what my parents and teachers taught me. That's all I need to know in this life. You are a non-caterpillar and that's that!"

"Homer, that sounded like your goodbye for today."

"Yes, goodbye for now, Caterfly, I've got to go home. Remember, if you have any trouble getting food, call me, I'll help you. Watch out for the non-caterpillars who eat caterpillars, they might mistake you for one and eat you. See you."

Homer disappeared down the limb toward the trunk of the cherry tree. His green body stood out starkly against the grey branch as he moved mechanically along.

"I don't know why he has any patience with me at

all," Caterfly thought. "He's been like a brother to me. I just can't accept his idea of the world as being either caterpillars or non-caterpillars. The mosquito I met last week described a hundred different creatures to me and named each one and all seemed to have a purpose in life." His train of thought was shattered by a loud voice.

"Caterfly, look up here," a commanding voice called sharply to him.

Narcis, a most beautiful brown and burnt orange butterfly was fluttering just above his branch and calling for his attention.

Caterfly raised his head just enough to see Narcis gracefully flutter about in the air before him.

"Narcis, I'm happy to see you again!"

"Caterfly, I hate to see you with your head drooping in unhappiness, but why do you insist on talking to caterpillars?"

"Some of them have been kind to me, that's why."

"Caterfly, they are depressing you because the more you associate with them, the more you think you are a caterpillar. You have wings you can never be a caterpillar. You are meant to fly like me, to be beautiful like me. Caterpillars are ugly and gross. You are meant to be like me, beautiful and perfect."

"Are you perfect, Narcis?"

"You bet I'm perfect! I can fly in the pure air; the caterpillars crawl in the filthy dirt of the ground and the trees. I don't crawl like those things. I'm pretty, not ugly. I'm sensitive to the subtleties of nature. Everything I do is beautiful and graceful, every creature knows that. Every creature envies me. I am the high point of nature."

"Just you, Narcis?"

"No, Caterfly, all of us butterflies are the highest form of life in the garden, and you can be like us if you just stop feeling sorry for yourself!" Narcis answered.

"How can I do that?"

"Fly. Beat your wings and fly, that's how!"

"Fly, Narcis? I've tried that before I'm too heavy to fly. I can't."

"Caterfly, don't say you can't. Your head is loaded up with negative ideas. You can fly. You can be a butterfly like me. Try it! Beat those wings!" Narcis shouted in encouragement.

Caterfly, who by this time was caught up in his friend's enthusiasm, beat his wings furiously for about a minute. The front half of his body left the branch for about a second, but the rest of his body stayed on the branch—immovable.

"I can't fly, I can't fly!" Caterfly cried loudly. "It's no use!"

"You can!" shouted Narcis. "The truth is you were flying. The front part of you, the butterfly, was flying. The rest of you held you to the branch."

"What is the rest of me?"

"I have an answer for that, Caterfly. After you were born—that is, after you fell out of the highest part of the sky with the rest of the butterflies—you must have hit a branch and knocked yourself out. While you were unconscious, a caterpillar tried to make a meal out of you. He succeeded in eating away the hind part of your body, but his head got stuck inside you. When you awoke, you thought he was part of your body. It makes sense, doesn't it?"

"How does he stay alive, Narcis?"

"When you eat, some of the food passes into his mouth which is jammed inside you and he eats as well. Caterfly, you are a butterfly with a real problem!"

Caterfly was silent for a long moment. Then he said, "How can I solve the problem?"

"Simple. You must kill the caterpillar and then you

will be free to be like me. If you are too squeamish to kill him, perhaps you could starve him a bit by not eating or batter him around until he leaves you."

Tears of gratitude filled Caterfly's eyes. Maybe he had the answer that would set him free and help him to find his true place in nature. "Thank you, Narcis. Thank you, thank you!" he exclaimed.

Narcis began to fly away backwards. "Caterfly, I must go now. I hope to see you flying in a few days. Take care, and good luck. Remember always you are a butterfly!"

As Narcis turned and fluttered away, an awed Caterfly watched him become invisible in the pink, red and orange flowers below.

Chapter 2

. . . in which a battered Caterfly decides to go in search of the light.

Homer was horrified by the condition in which he found Caterfly's body four days later. The wings and the emaciated body were battered, discolored, and deathlike.

Homer spent two days caring for his friend. He fed him some sweet nectar and water from his own mouth. He carried the life-giving substances from the blossoms he found a short distance from his weakened companion. At night, Homer tied him to the branch with a few strands of silk thread, since he feared Caterfly would lose his grip and be blown away while he slept.

On the third day, it rained. Since Caterfly wasn't strong enough to crawl any great distance for cover, Homer used a few cherry tree leaves to create a canopy over him. The leaves, too, were fastened in place by Homer's homespun silk thread.

At sunset on the fourth day of Caterfly's suffering, a welcome visitor crawled into his tent. Esmeralda, the caterpillar, snuggled up against the convalescent and spoke softly to him.

"Caterfly, Homer told me you were at death's door. I'm here to cheer you up! Tell me, what happened to you. You looked starved and all bruised up."

"Esmeralda, I am too embarrassed to talk about it, alright?"

Esmeralda answered him in a hurt voice. "Sure, it's alright with me if you tell Homer things and don't tell me . . . It's alright, really."

"Look, Esmeralda, I didn't tell Homer anything either. Somehow he knew better than to ask. I know you mean well, but I'd just like to forget some things."

The bright green insect did not speak to her recuperating companion for a minute. When she did speak, her voice seemed softer than usual.

"I understand what you mean by 'forget', Caterfly, I, too, have things to forget. I wasted half my life being fickle and proud. I've been quite a fool."

"Esmeralda, I'm beginning to believe that we are all fools. Some of us know this and some don't. Those who know it are a little less foolish than those who don't," Caterfly said pensively.

"What about those who don't know it?" she asked inquisitively.

"Those who don't see their own foolishness are dangerous. They kill us or cause us to kill ourselves, Esmeralda."

Caterfly turned his head away from Esmeralda. "I'd rather not talk about it, Esmeralda. That thought is painful."

"My poor dear, my poor mysterious Caterfly. Look at the glory of the rising sun, smell the lovely scents in the mild breeze, gaze upon the jubilant colors in our charming garden and you'll live and be happy, Caterfly."

Caterfly began to feel the loveliness of the day sweep over his entire being. His strength began to return as they watched the sun rise to noonday. For awhile he forgot who he was and what his problems were. He and Esmeralda whispered silly things to one another. As the hours passed, he felt ripples of happiness for the first time since he began asking questions about himself.

The sun's warmth had healed most of his aches and pains. Esmeralda snuggled close to him and radiated joy. The flowers of the garden seemed to grow softer and yet more brilliant than ever.

"I will live after all," he thought. "Maybe I'll be happy, too."

His delicate hopeful thoughts were interrupted by a nudge from Esmeralda. She spoke softly to him.

"Caterfly, do you like me?"

"Yes, I really do. You are beautiful and sweet," he said softly.

"I like you, Caterfly, I always did. I was always too shy to let you know—that is, until you got hurt. Do you like being around me . . . I mean . . . you aren't getting tired of me, are you?"

"Oh, no, Esmeralda, I like your being here!"

She waited for a few seconds to ask him, "How much do you like me?"

"Very much," he answered in a sincere tone.

"How much?" she repeated.

"Very, very much," he answered as his impatience grew.

There was a dead silence just before a cautious Esmeralda asked him, "Caterfly, do you love me?"

Another dead silence followed her question. The word love sounded too much like a commitment to a wary Caterfly. Long moments passed.

"Please answer me. Just tell me the truth and don't worry about hurting me," she gently insisted.

Everything was moving too fast for Caterfly. Images of his self-inflicted punishment and fasting began to cloud his mind.

After a brief pause, he responded in a firmer voice.

"Esmeralda, you asked for the truth. This is the truth—if I were to love anyone, it would be you. I could be very happy with you, but not at this time, because I don't know who I am, what I am, or what my purpose for living is. How can I love with all of my being if I have not answered any of these important questions yet?"

Esmeralda was obviously losing her patience with her blue and white insect companion. She raised her voice and said sharply, "Caterfly, don't be such a philosopher. Enjoy each day as it comes; that's all there is. Each day. Enjoy the days with me and I'll enjoy the nights with you. Feel the joy of life! A little to eat, a little to drink, and a lot of love and we'll pass our days in joy. Stop questioning and start enjoying your life. Things will work themselves out. Don't you see? You *need* me, Caterfly. Tell me you love me and everything will be alright." Esmeralda had been looking deeply into Caterfly's eyes as she spoke. Tears were forming in her own eyes.

Caterfly was deeply touched by her words. He was grateful that she wanted him to love her. "After all," he thought, "Maybe I should stop questioning things. The lovely garden is filled with pairs—pairs of birds, pairs of rabbits, pairs of bees, pairs of butterflies. Pairs, pairs, pairs! Maybe I'm only half of something greater and that's why I can't find answers. But, then again, I never saw a winged creature with a wingless one," he mused, "or a crawling one with a walking one, or one that burrows with one that hops." As he lost himself in thought, Esmeralda seemed to grow impatient.

"You are Caterfly; you are a caterpillar and your purpose is to love me and spend your days with me!"

"Esmeralda, I am not a caterpillar, but you might be right on the other two things you pointed out."

"You are a caterpillar, Caterfly. You are one of us.

Believe me, you are," Esmeralda sobbed.

"Esmeralda, I can't be a caterpillar because you want it to be so! For a few days I believed I was a butterfly, but I learned the hard way, I am just what I am—whatever that is."

"Do you realize that you contradict yourself, Caterfly? You are so confused that you don't make sense. Let me help you so that the confusion will end and we'll be happy together always . . . your wings must go, Caterfly! I'll ask my brother, Claude, to sever your wings."

"Sever my wings! Why?"

"Because without wings, you'll look and feel like a caterpillar. You'll accept yourself and spend your days loving me. Don't worry; I'll learn to love you more without your wings. Don't misunderstand, Caterfly, I would love you either way, but a female likes stability in a male. I wouldn't want you to fly away someday. It's not important to me to live out my life with the only flying caterpillar in the garden, but it is important to me that you become steady, realize your limitations. You must know what you are, so let my brother sever your wings. I'll arrange everything." She looked at him with determination and inspiration written in her face.

Caterfly felt anger and hurt rising within him from some hidden source. "Esmeralda, you just don't understand. I am my wings and my body, not just my body!"

A hurt Esmeralda replied, "You just can't make a sacrifice for me. You don't love me!"

Caterfly felt a rush of anger. He glared at his companion. "Sacrifice!" he shouted. "Maybe you should give up your thought that I must lose my wings to please you."

Esmeralda began to back away from him crying.

"Have I gone crazy? he thought. "I've hurt her feelings and she was only trying to help me." He calmed himself and said, "Look, Esmeralda, maybe we could work things out and at least be friends."

"Friendship!" she shouted. "I knew it. I mean nothing to you! Why don't you just admit it right now?"

He began to say, "Esmeralda, wait just a moment," but he only reached "Es . . ."by the time she had marched angrily away on all her tiny feet.

Night was falling as Caterfly watched Esmeralda disappear into some leaves on the branch above him.

He hadn't time to lose himself in thought before Homer's friendly voice called out to him in the darkness, "Caterfly, how do you feel?"

He forgot his loneliness as he answered in gratitude. "Homer, I'm healed up just fine, thanks to you and Esmeralda. You have been a tremendous help to me. I just wish there was some way I could repay you!"

"There is, Caterfly," Homer said as he emerged from the darkness. He faced Caterfly, "Just be happy, my friend . . . just be happy. Life is too short and beautiful to worry about anything. Hope in the future: where there is hope there is life."

For awhile, they rested themselves on the branch and watched the dazzling display of fireflies.

"Homer, what is that light out there? I've enjoyed watching it every night." Caterfly said.

"The moon, the stars, the fireflies what do you mean out there?"

"Homer, I mean the light at the eastern edge of our garden." Caterfly was staring at the small radiant white light at a great distance from the cherry tree.

"That's the light of mystery, Caterfly. No sense worrying about that, too," Homer said in an unconcerned tone.

"I'm not worried about it, Homer. Why do you call it the light of mystery?"

"It never moves, that's why. The moon moves, the

stars move, and the fireflies move, but the light of mystery never moves, that's why we call it a mystery. One thing for sure, it is a non-caterpillar."

"You know something, Homer, I really always have enjoyed watching it every night. Sometimes when I'm troubled, I watch it from sunset until dawn. It fascinates me."

"Caterfly, it is just some kind of light. There are a lot of things we don't understand. Why focus on that particular mystery?"

"Somehow, Homer, I think that light is part of me. That's what attracts me to it," Caterfly said in a firm voice.

"You forget, Caterfly, the world is either caterpillar or non-caterpillar. Nothing is really part of anything else."

The two insects continued their conversation into the deepening night amidst the glow of thousands of fireflies dancing in the air about them.

"Homer, you are a part of something, perhaps I am a part of something, too. Maybe there are others just like me somewhere in this garden - even one other!" New hope began to surge in Caterfly.

"Caterfly, the only real thing in this garden is this tree and the insects on it!" Homer said very emphatically.

"Homer, where do the flying creatures come from and where do they go?"

"They come from the clouds which are illusions built on the air, every creature knows that! I don't know where they go, since I was never taught that," Homer said calmly. Then he added, "That sort of thing isn't important to me, Caterfly."

"Homer, a few days ago, I saw a robin fly from this tree to that mulberry tree at the far end of the pond. The world is more than this tree, you must know that! How can you explain the pond below this tree. You've seen the fish in it stare up at you just as I have!"

"Nonsense. Every now and then our minds drift and we think we see things. This tree is the only real thing there is—all else is imaginary! All else is unknown!"

"The unknown suits me just fine, Homer, because I'm unknown even to myself. I welcome the unknown, since the known makes no sense to me. Tomorrow I'm leaving this tree and I'm going to travel to the mulberry tree," Caterfly said in a determined voice.

Homer was silent for a moment. He knew that Caterfly meant business. He didn't want to ask him to reconsider. He felt that Caterfly was going to die in his wild adventure into the unknown. He thought, "Perhaps this is the way out for my unfortunate friend, Caterfly. He will leave the tree and perish instantly and mercifully the way caterpillars perish in the beaks of birds."

"Caterfly, I just want you to know that I will miss you very much. Are you afraid?"

"Oh yes, Homer, I'm afraid, but even fear is a welcome change from the self-pity I've been wallowing in all my life."

A concerned Homer responded, "I'll leave you now, so that you can get your sleep and an early start tomorrow."

Homer felt he had to leave because thoughts of a dead Caterfly began to overwhelm him. He couldn't bear to look at his insect companion any longer. As he started to move away, he said quietly, "Good luck, Caterfly. Remember me when you get there."

Caterfly fought off tempting thoughts of staying as he watched his benefactor crawl into the night and disappear. He again turned his attention to the light at the eastern end of the garden while he thought about the possibilities and dangers he might encounter on his great adventure. His last thought just before falling asleep was, "The world must be bigger than this tree, it *has* to be!"

Chapter 3

. . . in which he meets a singing frog.

The warm rays of the morning sun roused Caterfly into wakefulness. He immediately began the descent down his branch of the cherry tree on to the main trunk. Out of sight a tearful Homer watched his friend's every step. Caterfly seemed so small and pathetic to Homer as he inched further and further away from his home.

A few large black worker ants brushed past the blue and white insect just before he completed his descent and crawled onto the ground at the base of the tree. He was confused by the strange sensation of crawling on earth rather than tree bark.

"Will it support my weight?" he wondered. "Will I sink through it into a bottomless pit like the hole in the trunk that all insects fear? It must be solid," he thought, "or how could it support the tree?" He felt more confidence as he left the area of the trunk and plunged through the sea of grass that grew below the towering brightly colored flowers that seemed to be everywhere.

Homer watched him closely for as long as he could see the least sign of his friend's blue and white body and wings. Finally Caterfly disappeared into the grass and flowers below. "It's all over now." Homer thought sadly. "It's for the best. Such a tragedy either way," he thought. "Living or dying for my friend was so sad," Homer sobbed. Homer sat on the lowest branch of the cherry tree and wept as Caterfly held his wings close to his body and crawled as quickly as he could away from the tree toward the unknown.

Caterfly navigated through the dense terrain by using his scent of water to keep the pond at his right as he moved ahead. Following the pond away from his cherry tree home would lead to the tree he had observed at the other end of the pond—a tree that he could no longer see through the roof and corridors of abundantly growing flowers and wild grass. Caterfly began to enjoy his journey. The ground was solid; his new world was filled with beautiful scents and exciting variations of colors.

From time to time he observed some strange insects dart through the tall grass in pursuit of food. The strong scent of the pond guided him through the grass forest to the bank of the tranquil pond itself. Caterfly paused for a minute to get his sense of directions. Far in the distance, he could see his objective. He turned around and viewed the tree of his departure standing close by in all its flowering loveliness.

"I didn't make much progress at all," he thought.

"Sunset will find me less than a quarter of the distance to my goal. I can't worry about it."

As he began to plod his way along the bank toward the ever distant goal, he was amused by a strange sight. A small frog was sitting on a branch and paddling his way through the lotus flowers in the pond. The frog was mockingly singing, "Row, row, row your boat—life is but an empty dream," as he approached his smiling observer.

"If life is but an empty dream, why row your boat?" Caterfly called out to him.

The frog rammed his small barge into the soft bank and sat staring at Caterfly for a long moment. He said calmly, "Young Sir, your remark is as absurd as your appearance. Just what species of beast are you?"

"Whatever I am I seem to be a one-of-a-kind beast. Can you answer my question?" Caterfly laughed.

"First of all, youngster, you are not a one-of-a-kind beast," the frog stated flatly.

"I'm not!" Caterfly exclaimed.

"No, nature is always trying to evolve its creatures into something better—that is something that can crawl better, run faster, fly higher and so on. The whole idea is stupid because everything ends up dead anyway so there's no sense to the whole thing. Do you see what I mean?"

Caterfly was a little disappointed. He had hoped to gain information on a creature like himself, instead the frog told him his view on how stupid life seemed to be. He managed to ask, "Then what makes us try to better ourselves, Mr. Frog?"

"It's some absurd instinct nature put in us so that it can continue its stupid game that's why, Mr. Inquisitive Beast. I used to be a tadpole, now I'm a frog. I was happier as a tadpole."

"Why?" Caterfly asked.

"Because now I have more freedom."

Caterfly was puzzled. "But that's great," he said.

"No, it's even more absurd, because now I don't even know what to do with my freedom. Should I go under water and be eaten by a large fish or should I go on land to be gobbled up by the beasts of the land or the vicious birds?"

"Certainly Mr. Frog, there must be some advantages to your evolution?"

"Yes, I've fully learned how stupid nature and evolution really are. You should know what I mean. You are somewhere between a caterpillar and a butterfly. You are both, but at the same time you are neither. You are another proof of nature's absurd attempts to evolve creatures into something better. Nature is making billions of attempts every day and all of her attempts end in absurdity, failure, and death," the frog concluded with a smug smiling face.

Caterfly was momentarily overwhelmed by the frog's confident remarks.

"You'll have to excuse me, youngster, but I see some flies down there." Still facing Caterfly, the frog pushed his raft away from the bank and began to paddle while he sang a variation of his tune.

"Row, row, row your life,
gently down the emptiness,
merrily, merrily, merrily, merrily
life is but an empty pond."

Caterfly rested as he watched the frog paddle his branch barge around a bend in the distance.

"I must be brave," he thought. "I must be brave no matter what he said. He could be wrong, too." He moved ahead toward the tree in the distance. He munched a little on some fallen leaves as they appeared on the path he had plotted for his journey. He climbed into the lower branches of a small bush as night fell. He was so fascinated by the strange pond sounds and the new insect voices he heard that night that he didn't bother to look for the light at the end of the garden. His many legs got a good grip on his branch of the bush and he fell into a deep sleep.

Chapter 4

. . . in which Caterfly rides like the wind on Harry, The Rat.

On the morning of the second day of his journey, Caterfly drove himself as hard as he could for more than five hours. He ate and drank on the move so he would lose no time. During the sixth hour of his trek, he exhausted himself trying to push through the extremely heavy grass which grew down to the water's edge.

He considered taking an alternative route, but discarded that plan for fear of getting out of range of the ponds' scent. If he lost the scent of the pond, he would be lost. He decided to rest for an hour in the nearest clump of grass. As he rested, he pondered his chances of getting through the grass wall ahead. He was startled by a huge pair of black eyes staring wildly at him through his grass couch.

The eyes protruded from a furry grey head.

"A rat!" Caterfly shrieked.

"Are you edible, little fellow?" The rat inquired through his terribly sharp teeth.

Caterfly was frightened, but he managed to say, "No sir, Mr. Rat, I'm a rare breed of poisonous insect."

Before responding, the rat pushed his snout a little closer to Caterfly and turned the open side of his ears toward him. "You look poisonous, alright." The rat said sniffing the blue and white insect a little. "What are you doing in my territory, strange one? Don't worry I won't eat you. I'm pretty selective about my diet contrary to common opinion!"

"Thank you, Mr. Rat. I'm sorry that I entered your territory, but I really didn't know it was yours."

"You are stupid!" he snapped. "Didn't you know that every creature has his own territory and this area had to belong to some creature—that's what it's all about!"

"Yes, I'm stupid, Mr. Rat," Caterfly said most apologetically. "I'm a creature but I don't hold any territory of my own so I assumed my way was the way of other creatures in the world."

"The world? The world! What do you know about the world! The world is territory—killing for territory and having pleasure in your own territory—that's all! You aren't another rat I must kill for my land nor are you a predator that would kill me for my territory. What are you?" As the rat spoke his fur went up on his neck as he backed away from the mysterious insect. He held his body in a well balanced position ready to pounce or run, depending on Caterfly's reaction to his question.

Caterfly couldn't restrain his laughter.

The outburst of laughter further confused the rat who started to bear his terrible teeth.

"Mr. Rat, I'm not a rat. You know that by my scent."

The rat began to back away from the relatively tiny insect. All his movements were guarded.

Caterfly restrained his laughter since he felt a great sympathy for the way the rat was locked within his own instincts. Aside from his sympathy, he wanted to stay alive and reach his goal. "Maybe Mr. Rat could help me," he thought.

"Mr. Rat," he said in a respectful voice, "my name is Caterfly. I'm the most dangerous creature in the garden for those who fear the unknown."

The rat braced himself again.

"Caterfly, are you a predator?"

"Now listen Mr. Rat and don't run! I only prey upon the unknown, not rats. If a rat ate me he would grow very sick and die. Do we understand one another?"

"If you are not here to make a meal out of me" the rat said in a friendly tone, "then you can call me Harry."

"O.K. Harry," Caterfly said in a relieved tone.

"I can't figure you out, Caterfly. What are you doing in my territory? Do you want to settle here . . . huh? It's o.k. with me—I mean since we're not natural enemies. I won't bother you and you won't bother me. We're different, but we could have a truce. Do you understand?"

"Yes, I do, Harry, but I'll be moving along."

"Where? To find a territory?"

"Yes, you might say that, Harry," Caterfly answered softly.

"Where will your territory be, Caterfly" Harry asked.

"It will be where I understand myself, Harry," he answered.

"Which direction are you headed, Caterfly?" the rat asked as he grew more puzzled than ever about the insect.

"Through the heavy grass ahead, Harry. About five day's march to that tree at the end of the pond."

Harry, the rat, laughed. "I know the tree you mentioned. It's a mulberry tree and you could fly there in two hours. Five days . . . nonsense!"

"Harry, you don't understand. I can't fly."

"You're a flying bug who can't fly at all, but you're willing to struggle through the high grass until you find your territory or until you die. Is that right?" Harry said with new understanding in his voice.

"Yes, that's right Harry. That's it exactly," Caterfly answered.

"You've got guts, Caterfly. You *do* know what it's all

about—territory. I'm willing to fight to the death for my territory and you're willing to die to get to yours. You're okay, Caterfly."

"Thank you, Harry."

"Too bad you're not a rat, Caterfly."

"Why Harry?"

"Because a good rat could make it to that mulberry tree in five minutes, that's why."

"That's impossible!" Caterfly laughed, since the idea seemed inconceivable to him.

"Impossible eh? Impossible? I'll show you. I'll run up to the tree and back in ten minutes. That should show you that Harry, the rat, is faster than he is commonly believed to be. Watch this," Harry said as he turned in the direction of the mulberry tree.

At that moment Caterfly shouted to him, "Harry, don't do it!"

"Why not?" the rat answered sharply.

"Because I won't be able to see if you make it to the tree from my position here." An idea was forming in the insect's brain.

"I can do it I tell you!"

"There is a way you could show me, Harry, and if you could make the tree in five minutes, I'd be willing to tell all the creatures in the garden that you are the fastest creature in the garden."

"Tell me how, Caterfly, just tell me how I could show you so that you could tell the world!" Harry exclaimed.

"Well, Harry, carry me on your back as you run. I'll hold on and you'll run as fast as you can to the tree."

"Excellent idea, little bug! You're so light I'll make it easily."

As Caterfly left his resting place and began to position himself on Harry's back, the rat turned his head to see if everything was alright.

"Everything okay, Caterfly?"

"Yes, Harry. Thank you."

"It will be your responsibility to hang on. I can't run fast and worry at the same time—if you know what I mean."

"Yes, Harry, I understand."

"You watch the stations of the sun and count off the minutes, okay Caterfly? I mean I can't worry about time and run fast at the same time—alright?

"Alright, Harry."

"No talking during the run, okay? I mean . . ."

"Okay Harry," Caterfly impatiently interrupted.

"Listen Caterfly, my territory ends about half a minute's run from the tree—so I'll run up to the end of my territory in four and a half minutes and that should prove that I could make it to the tree in five minutes—alright Caterfly?"

"Yes, yes, that's proof enough Harry!"

"Thank you. Little bug, are you ready?"

"Yes!"

As he heard the word "yes" Harry took off with a great burst of speed through the tall grass. Caterfly clutched at his fur for dear life. Harry's speed increased as he ran crazily around the larger clumps of grass and leaped through smaller clumps. Caterfly held his wings close to his body as the pace quickened. The scents came and went faster than the insect's little brain could register them. The grassland became a blur of greens, yellows, and browns.

Harry's pace increased alarmingly, but he showed no signs of tiring whatsoever. Every now and then a blade of grass battered Caterfly and almost unseated him, but he tightened his grip with all the strength at his command. When the blue and white rider looked above, the sun seemed to jump about in the sky. At times he could see reflections from the pond appear and disappear on his right.

"Two minutes to go, Harry!" he shouted. Harry quickened his pace. He was running incredibly fast. Everything became a blur for Caterfly. He grabbed Harry's whiskers which were beating wildly against his face and tightened his grip. Nothing seemed to register plainly in his brain. The rushing air caused by Harry's speed threatened to suffocate the gasping insect. Insects of all sorts seemed to be spinning out of the path of Harry, the projectile. Strange sounds and colors spun in the insects brain. Forms of birds and large animals seemed to appear and disappear as the mad race against time continued.

"Half a minute to go!" Shouted Caterfly half fearing that his words would spur his steed to yet greater speeds.

Almost immediately after hearing the time, Harry began to slow his pace. After a few seconds more had elapsed, he began to trot proudly.

"There it is, Caterfly," he said calmly.

Caterfly cleared his whirling head and joyfully observed the mulberry tree about a half minute's rat run ahead.

"It's so beautiful!" he shouted with joy. "The cherry tree was just part of a bigger world; I knew it!" Tears filled his eyes. "Oh thank you, Harry. You are indeed the greatest runner in all the world!"

A delighted Harry flattened himself on the ground to help his rider dismount more easily.

Caterfly dismounted without great difficulty and was amazed that Harry, the rat, didn't seem the least bit tired.

"You understand, Caterfly, that this is as far as I can go—this is the boundary of my territory. Between us

and the mulberry tree is a territory belonging to another rat family. I wouldn't want to tangle with them by invading their territory. I couldn't begin to tell you how many bloody fights rat families have in order to decide these boundaries. You know what I mean?"

Caterfly looked about but couldn't see any boundary markers. "Harry, where are the markers?" he asked.

"The boundaries are only in our minds, Caterfly. Do you understand?"

"Yes, I understand now, Harry."

"Well, Caterfly, thank you."

"For what, Harry?" Caterfly was filled with gratefulness and surprise at Harry's thank you.

"Thank you, little bug, for helping me to have some fun today. That was enjoyable."

"It was great fun, Harry, thank you too."

Harry, the rat, faced Caterfly once again. "Goodbye brave little fellow and good luck with your territory."

"Goodbye, Harry." Caterfly answered. "Someday I hope to see you again."

"If you don't come to see me again, Caterfly, I'll know why. You'll be somewhere else defending your territory."

Caterfly would have liked to talk longer, to ask him a hundred questions about a rat's life, but Harry bounded away through the tall grass in a strictly business-like manner.

Chapter 5

. . . wherein he lives through the terrible attacks of ravenous birds and encounters Black Jack.

Caterfly focused his attention on the mulberry tree as he crawled at his best speed toward it. "If only Homer were with me now," he thought. "He'd see that there is a world outside of his world."

When he was very close to the trunk of the tree, he was stopped by a small brown ant.

"Where are you going, brother?" the brown ant asked him.

"I'm going up the tree", Caterfly answered him cautiously.

"Might I ask why you are going up the tree?"

"I have personal business up there," Caterfly answered more confidently. Caterfly hoped that "personal business" would be taken by the ant to mean that he was backed up by friends who were waiting above. He didn't want to invite an attack from a squad of food-gathering ants. He knew ants wouldn't be fooled by his "poisonous insect" story.

"I'm sorry if I seem to be prying into your business, brother, but I ask you these questions to help you."

"To help me?" Caterfly asked.

"If you
listen closely,
you will hear
some frightening
sounds above.
Birds are attacking
the insects up there."
Caterfly listened
intently. Sure enough,
he heard the screams
of caterpillars and the
delighted shrieks of birds.
The sounds made him shiver with fright.

"Thank you for warning me," he said.

"If you climb the tree, brother, you won't have much
of a chance to survive. If you stay on the ground with
me, I'll get you a good job," the brown ant said in a
helpful voice.

"A job?"

"Yes, a job. My name is Bruce, and my job is to find good workers for Antdom, the society of brown ants. At times, ants use the services of other insects and in return we feed and protect them. Our war with the red ants has depleted our labor force. Frankly, we could certainly use you. Some of the labor captains are short sighted in this matter, but once they try other insects on their labor gangs, they're usually convinced that it's a good idea."

"I appreciate your offer, Bruce, and I might seem selfish to you, but I've journeyed a long way to reach this tree and I must climb it no matter what," a determined Caterfly answered.

"I won't argue that point," Bruce said. "You must be conscientious to carry on personal business in the face of such danger. Look me up if you ever change your mind. By the way, what's your name?"

"Caterfly," the blue and white insect answered softly. "It was nice talking to you, Bruce, but I must be on my way."

"Good luck, Caterfly!" Bruce shouted as the determined insect cautiously began to ascend the trunk.

As Caterfly climbed halfway up the mulberry tree, he was horrified by a clear view of the chilling spectacle above. Dozens of birds of various types were fluttering wildly about the tree devouring caterpillars by the hundreds as they hopelessly tried to avoid the murderous beaks which pierced them.

Some of the birds were walking along the branches, beating their wings for balance while they greedily gobbled up every caterpillar in sight. Other, smaller birds, flew crazily along the branches pecking violently at slow moving caterpillars and devouring them as quickly as they could. Some birds flew to and fro from the tree carrying other victims to their hungry families.

As Caterfly reached the undersection of the lowest branch of the tree, he could painfully hear the pathetic squealing of the frightened insects even above the loud screeching of the birds of prey. He was momentarily stunned by the horror show. "Maybe Homer was right; this can't be real," he thought.

"Get under cover, you idiot!" a shrill, piercing voice stabbed into his consciousness.

Caterfly, startled by the command, looked up at a small hole in the trunk just above his branch. A black spider beckoned to him from the aperture. "If you want to save your life, get in here fast!"

Caterfly crawled a little closer to the hole and looked the spider squarely in his eyes. "Don't give me that stuff, spider. I'm no fool! You've got a web in there to trap me. You care as much about me as these murdering birds!"

Just as Caterfly was completing his statement, a robin swooped past the underside of the first branch and flew away with a bright green caterpillar that had been hiding there.

"Listen, you nut, I don't know what you are, but you don't look very edible to me. At least take a look in here before you decide to die out there. I don't have a web in here. See for yourself," the spider shouted.

"A friendly spider?" Caterfly said mockingly as the robin swooped by again and picked off another caterpillar near him.

"I'm too slow to retreat down the trunk," he thought.

"I'm dead if I stay here. I'll take a look. What do I have to lose?" he thought as he inched his way toward the dark hole as the spider backed inside. The spider was half Caterfly's size; this gave the winged insect confidence.

Caterfly peered into the spider's sanctuary. There was no web in the hole. The hole seemed to widen at the base, but there was no web at the bottom either. A sparrow landed on the branch and began to walk quickly toward Caterfly. The desperate insect thrust himself into the hole. Within two seconds, the sparrow jammed its beak in the hole jabbing it about in a frenzied probe to find the frightened insect.

Caterfly remained still in a small crevice inside the pit. The sparrow quickly grew impatient, since much crawling food awaited him within easy reach outside the hole.

When the beaked head disappeared, the hole filled with bright sunlight, and Caterfly observed the spider move toward him. He wanted to say something to discourage any maneuver on the part of his possible enemy.

"Mr. Spider, before you move any closer, let me tell you something."

The black leggy insect stopped all movements.

"I realize you have a stinger and can sting me to death, but your poison takes time to work. Before I die, I'll drag you outside, and the birds will eat both of us!" Caterfly threatened.

"You ingrate!" the spider shouted. "You lousy ingrate! I've saved your life and shared my home with you. Instead of thanking me, you treat me like a murderer."

Caterfly was speechless from the electric reaction of the spider. He remained silent and motionless not knowing what to say next.

"Listen, stranger, I don't know who you are, but if you knew me, you'd know I have a reputation around here for being honest and sincere."

The frightened screams and screeching grew louder outside the small sanctuary.

Caterfly didn't know why, but he felt irritated by the spider's self-praise.

"Mr. Spider", he said.

"You can call me Black Jack," the spider said coldly.

"Alright, call me Caterfly. Black Jack, are you trying to tell me you are not a murderer?"

"Caterfly, if I'm a murderer, you're a murderer as much as those birds out there are murderers," he said sharply.

"What do you mean I'm a murderer?" Caterfly demanded in a shocked tone.

"Let's define terms," the spider said.

Caterfly agreed, "Go ahead."

"A murderer is one who deliberately and directly kills an innocent. Do you agree?"

"Yes, that sounds good. That's what those murdering birds are doing right now and that's what you do, Black Jack, when you catch insects in your web and eat them! Yes, I accept your definition."

"Caterfly, would you say that a plant is alive?"

"Yes, of course," the blue and white striped insect answered.

"You eat plants?"

"Yes, but that's different," Caterfly said in a wavering voice.

"How?" Black Jack said confidently.

"Because I have to eat to stay alive!" Caterfly responded.

"Well, I suppose you think I don't have the same problem!" Black Jack said sarcastically.

"No, a plant is a lower form of life; you eat higher forms of life—us insects—insects, in some ways like yourself," Caterfly said with renewed confidence.

"Caterfly, can you prove that a plant is less innocent than an insect? Can you prove that an insect is a higher form of life than a plant? How can you justifiably say such a thing? You are so loaded up with preconceived ideas, it's tragic."

Caterfly's insect brain whirled, but he couldn't find handy proofs for his statement. He could tell the spider that he was just stating what he had heard from other insects, but that would do no good. He thought, "Am I merely justifying my preying upon plant life as Black Jack is justifying preying upon insect life?" Caterfly was very confused.

He said, "Well, at least I don't carefully plan my killings."

"You mean my web?" the black leggy spider laughed.

"Yes, your web is a preconceived murder instrument."

"Tell me truthfully, Caterfly, does it make you feel better to know that you kill because your belly drives you to do so instead of your brain?"

Caterfly remained silent, thinking.

"You are indeed a prejudiced insect, Caterfly. You don't know the real purpose of my life or my web which is an expression of my beliefs. My web is beautiful in its logic and logical in its beauty. Beauty and logic, logic and beauty—what more can an insect hope to attain in his short life span? You tell me."

Caterfly thought for a moment and answered, "Black Jack, your beauty and logic kills. How can true beauty and logic kill? You tell me."

"Caterfly, Caterfly, your mind is so dark and ignorant," the spider said sympathetically. "I create the web because I love order and beauty. I do not cause the insects to fly into my web, which after all is my life and my property! If I kill, I kill indirectly to maintain my instincts. You kill plant life directly to maintain your instincts. Who is the greater murderer?"

Caterfly remained silent.

"I add logic and beauty to the world I take my daily food from. What do you do except destroy leaves and other green things? What do you create? Tell me, Caterfly. Tell me," the spider said mockingly.

In a quiet voice, Caterfly answered, "I wish I had an answer for you, Black Jack. I don't know what to say."

"I like you, Caterfly," the spider said as he moved close to his debate opponent and patted his head with three of his spindly black legs. "You are pretty honest, and it's hard to find an honest insect these days."

Suddenly, the extreme silence of the outside world became dramatically apparent to the two insects who were hiding from the bird attack.

"They're gone," said Caterfly in a relieved voice.

"Yes, the outside danger is gone, but what about the dangers inside us?" the spider replied.

"The darkness inside me is what drove me to leave my home, Black Jack," the winged insect answered.

"You mean the darkness of what you are and what your purpose is," said the spider full of understanding.

"Yes, exactly."

"Well, you know that the purpose of my life is logic and beauty, but maybe I too am full of prejudice when I think that my purpose should be your purpose, Caterfly," the spider said in a kind voice.

"Black Jack, don't you ever have any doubts about your beliefs?"

"Frankly, sometimes I do, Caterfly, but when doubts appear, I work harder and harder and make bigger and better webs," he said.

"Why?"

"Working helps me forget my problems. Maybe all problems can't be solved anyway. I would soon starve if I let my problems and questions about myself run my life. Do I make sense to you?"

"Yes, Black Jack, I understand your view," said Caterfly, who was beginning to view his problems as insurmountable.

"Please come with me," the spider motioned Caterfly outside.

They crawled out of the hole together and along the lowest branch to a magnificent spider's web which graced the space between the lowest branch and the one above. The web was an astounding feat of engineering and beauty. The pattern itself was amazingly intricate. The net was made with enough slack to sway with the moving branches.

"It's just beautiful," Caterfly gasped.

"Thank you. I am quite an engineer and an artist to boot," the spider said proudly.

"Yes, you are, Black Jack. I've never seen anything so wonderful and deadly created by any living creature."

"Deadly? Are you still on that kick, Caterfly?" the spider said in mock anger.

Caterfly remained quiet.

"Notice, Caterfly, I created a work which is a thousand times bigger than myself! Maybe if you found some work to do, you might find happiness that way. I'm sure you could create something lovely out of your life if you tried."

"Yes, maybe you're right, Black Jack, but I don't seem to have your ability," Caterfly said as he looked with awe at the web swaying in the mild breeze.

The spider responded sharply, "Certainly you have some ability—use it! Build something! Work!"

"I appreciate your encouragement, but I seem to have alternatives to work built into my instincts. You don't seem to have that problem," Caterfly said.

"Nonsense, Caterfly, I could have taken an easy way out when I was when I was small."

"What do you mean?" a surprised Caterfly answered.

"Ballooning, that's what I mean!"

"Ballooning? I don't understand," Caterfly said as he struggled to comprehend the strange concept.

"You see, you don't know anything about spiders—just as I suspected. Many of my young pals used their silken threads to make long cords and suspended themselves from the cords until a wind carried them to who knows where," he said in a matter-of-fact tone.

"Incredible!" exclaimed Caterfly. "Where did they go?"

"In the direction of the wind. In the direction of adventure. Who knows?"

"How exciting," Caterfly exclaimed again. "To fly off in adventure! To blow away into the unknown!"

"Your mind is drifting away, Caterfly. Find some useful work and you'll probably find yourself," Black Jack stated flatly.

Caterfly listened intently as the black spider explained his web-making technique to him. Their conversation on the web continued until nightfall.

As it grew darker, Caterfly observed that the light at the far end of the garden seemed much brighter than ever before. The two insects watched the luminescence grow through the center of the web.

"Yes, Caterfly, I love the light too. I love it so much that I used it to center my web. My work is directly centered on the light."

"It's much brighter here than where I came from, Black Jack."

"It will always be out of reach, Caterfly."

"If it is larger here because I've been moving toward it, won't it be larger up ahead?" Caterfly said hopefully, pointing at the light with his right wing.

"It will always be out of reach, Caterfly, why worry about it?"

"Black Jack, I believe that the light is part of me somehow," Caterfly said softly.

"Yes, I know what you mean, but it is just another

mystery that we can never explain. This is all the more reason why you need work to take your mind off of all troublesome mysteries."

Caterfly thought for a moment before speaking.

"Yes, maybe you're right, Black Jack! This work idea is worth a try. Tomorrow I'll look for work. Some ants down below need some help. Maybe, I could be of service to them, at least."

"Yes, why not?" the black spider said happily. Black Jack felt that he had helped his confused winged companion to find himself. "Just promise me that someday soon you'll come back and let me know how you're doing. Fair enough?"

"Fair enough, Black Jack. I'm sorry about the insults and trouble I gave you."

"Nonsense, we spiders have been given a bad name by the other insects. Most insects never listen to our side of the story. They're too frightened by us to try to understand our beliefs. I'm always delighted to have a good conversation with any creature. I see good in all creatures, don't you?"

Thinking of the vicious attacks of the birds upon the helpless insects, Caterfly answered, "Not yet, Black Jack, not yet."

They fell asleep side by side on the lower branch of the mulberry tree in the cool breeze of the garden. The stars and the lightening bugs danced and twinkled in the darkness. The only other sources of light were the moon and the radiance at the center of the web.

Chapter 6

. . . in which Caterfly, with the help of a true friend, balloons high and wide across the world.

"Well, I'm happy to hear you want to work with us," said a delighted Bruce, the brown ant, to Caterfly the next morning at the base of the mulberry tree.

"I'll give it a try," said Caterfly.

"Oh Captain, oh Captain Bos!" shouted Bruce to the leader of a large group of worker ants slowly moving a dead grasshopper past Bruce and Caterfly.

"Keep moving!" shouted Bos to his command of workers as he turned and crawled toward the voice that was beckoning to him.

"Yeah, what do you want, Bruce? You know I don't like to be disturbed when I'm on the job."

"Bos, this is Caterfly. I just wanted to introduce you two," Bruce said smilingly.

"If Caterfly is food, fine! I have no time to socialize," Bruce said sharply. "There is work to be done. What do you want?" he said, squarely eyeing Caterfly.

Caterfly trembled a little since he didn't appreciate being appraised for food value, and the captain seemed to be sizing him up for that purpose. "I want to work with you!" Caterfly said sharply.

Without batting his eyes or showing the least surprise, the captain said, "Unheard of," turned and began to crawl away.

"Captain!" Bruce shouted, "Caterfly is five times bigger than any ant. Even if he could only haul five times his own weight, he could do the work of twenty-five ants!"

Bos stopped and turned to face Caterfly again.

Bruce continued, "At this time, you need laborers more than food, captain. Give Caterfly a chance. Ants have used other insects for labor. Use Caterfly for labor. Use Caterfly, captain, and he will increase your efficiency."

"Let's go, Caterfly," Bos snapped.

Caterfly thanked Bruce and crawled quickly after the captain who soon overtook the group of ants struggling to transport the mammoth grasshopper to their territory. More than forty ants were pulling and pushing the giant at an obviously painful pace.

Caterfly requested the captain to inform his command that he was to be regarded as a common laborer, not as food. After the captain communicated the message to the amazed laborers by shouting it to them, Caterfly joined the group and began to push the grasshopper with his nose. He tried not to think about how the grasshopper met his death. He didn't want to view his new associates as killers. He felt more comfortable regarding them as foragers of food instead. He pushed the dead insect about a foot when the complaints of the laborers became boisterous.

The captain noticed that Caterfly's wings seemed to

get in the way of the ants as they moved forward and that he was accidently stepping on the others due to his awkward size. He just didn't seem to fit in the team of workers. He was about to tell Caterfly he was fired when the blue and white striped insect shouted, "Wait a minute, Captain! Wait a minute!"

"You want a minute break already? You lazy thing!" the captain shouted angrily.

"No, captain, listen!" Caterfly shouted as he stopped pushing the insect. Put the load on my back and I'll carry it alone."

The captain and his laborers were stunned by the incomprehensible idea. "Impossible!" the captain laughed. "Your idea is so impossible, it deserves a try."

The ants immediately loaded the grasshopper on Caterfly's back, between his wings.

When the ants climbed off his body, Caterfly began to crawl forward with his monstrous load. The ants cheered his progress. Caterfly moved ahead at his best speed, balancing the dead insect between his wings as he proceeded.

The relieved ants crawled quickly on his flanks. As they moved alongside the struggling Caterfly, they encouraged him by chanting, "Bravo, bravo, strong Caterfly! Bravo, bravo, strong Caterfly!" Sounds of joyful singing filled the air.

The captain felt elated as he led the procession yard after yard through the grassy plain ahead toward the ant village.

Happiness filled Caterfly as he labored for the first time in his life. "So this is work?" he thought happily. "This is work! Sweet is labor; sweet are the fruits of work. I'm accepted here, I'm respected here—me—Caterfly!" Such were his thoughts as he dutifully carried his burden hour after hour under the direction of the captain.

When he was within sight of the many mounds of the ant kingdom, Caterfly noticed that Bos was exchanging recognition signals through his antennae to various sentries as they proceeeded.

Finally, scores of worker ants from the many mounds removed Caterfly's burden and began to systematically dismantle it. Mechanical grating and grinding sounds filled the air.

Caterfly shivered as he heard the sounds over the shouts of many captains and supervisors.

"It's their food, after all," he thought. "They don't have any other way to survive. They've been decent to me. Maybe the grasshopper attacked them. Who knows for sure? The ants seem reasonable enough. They work so hard, they're so efficient—they can't be that bad."

"Caterfly!" captain Bos interrupted the insect's thoughts.

"I've enjoyed working with you," the captain said smilingly.

Caterfly was puzzled, since Bos seemed to be saying goodbye.

Bos continued, "I delivered that grasshopper so quickly I was promoted! I'm going far to the eastern end of the garden to set up supplies for our fourth army which is fighting the red army that has been stealing our eggs and forcing our young to serve them as slaves. You will be assigned to a new captain tomorrow morning. Good luck!"

A surprised Caterfly watched a happy captain Bos trot quickly away.

During the following week, Caterfly faithfully served various masters. Each captain he served was promoted. Ant captain vied with ant captain to use Caterfly in his work force. The blue and white striped insect became a specialist in moving the larger dead insects. Caterfly immersed himself in the joy of work. He forgot himself and thought only of the happiness he derived from his labors. Everywhere in the brown ant kingdom he was praised secretly and openly by the masters and the laborers alike.

On the seventh day of his new life, his group came upon the object to be moved a little too soon. The killer group had not yet finished its work. Caterfly was shocked by the ugly spectacle before him. A small frog was twisting and turning under a boiling sea of brown ants. The frog's shouts shattered all of Caterfly's illusions about his job. He had never wanted to confront the death scene of the creatures he carried. He wanted to break and run, but he checked himself. He wished that his group hadn't moved so quickly through the grasslands. It was one thing to transport a dead creature, it was another to watch it die.

When the struggle ended, the killer horde quickly fled the scene to their next assignment. As the tiny frog was loaded on his back, Caterfly could feel its warmth against his body. He thought of the frog he met rowing along the pond's shimmering surface.

"Life is but an empty nightmare," he murmured as he began to make headway under his heavy load.

"Why a frog?" he asked a fellow laborer on his right.

"War!" was the reply. "More food is needed now. They'll kill anything possible for them to kill. Soon, when things grow even worse, they'll kill you, too, Caterfly."

"Me!" he shuddered.

"Yes, you. When war gets tough enough, we eat our friends as well as our enemies. You should know that!"

"I just want to work, that's all," responded Caterfly.

"We all just want to work," a laborer to his left murmured. "War won't give us work, it can only give us death in the end—that's all."

At times, as the labor force proceeded, the weight of the dead frog caused Caterfly to stop in weariness. The workers during those times would run ahead of him and try to clear the ground of obstacles. Trying to encourage him they chanted:

"Caterfly the Strong,
Caterfly the Great,
Caterfly our friend"

over and over again to give him courage to continue his Herculean task.

When the food party returned to their village, there were no cheers to greet them. About a thousand brown ants were running riot about the domes. The broken bodies of hundreds of entangled red and brown ants lay in heaps near the ant hills. Captains shouted their orders to laborers and soldier ants that were crazily running about searching for the enemy.

As his laborer friends eased the dead frog from his back, he heard one say to the other, "The red ants raided our tunnels this time. We stopped their raiding party, but the war is getting worse and worse."

Incredible as it seemed to Caterfly, within two hours the ant village was once again the scene of neatness and order. There was not a trace of death anywhere; even the frog had been dismantled and its parts pulled out of sight.

"There is only an illusion of peace here," he thought. "Why should I allow myself to be comforted by illusions? What do I really know about these ants? Are they really any different than the smaller red ants? Where is this kingdom going? Do I really want to go with them? Did I journey this far just to be a carter of dead bodies?" a troubled Caterfly thought.

The day's duties had brought with them much self doubt and lack of peace for Caterfly. He decided to learn more about his adopted society in order to clear his insect head. He began to crawl slowly toward an ant school nearby.

"If only today hadn't happened," he thought. "I almost did find myself by losing myself in work, but something is wrong somewhere. Work always seems to be a part of something else—some higher purpose. What happens if the higher purpose has less value than the work itself? I love work, but I have violence. I even tried lying to myself, but I'm unhappy again. What does work mean to me? What does work mean to these ants? What does life mean to these ants? What does life mean to me?"

With troubled thoughts, Caterfly followed a group of young students to an open air school under a wild red rose which grew in the center of the ant village.

Since Caterfly loomed more than five times bigger than any student, the elderly principal of the school requested him to remain in the rear of the one classroom that was in operation that day. The principal then ran to the front of the classroom, crawled to the top of a pebble and shouted at the noisy, milling youngsters.

"Quiet! Quiet! There must be quiet or you won't learn anything at all!"

Caterfly was amazed how quickly the three hundred students grew silent. He noticed that some of the little heads turned, however, and tiny eyes shot him backward glances.

After the principal silenced the crowd, the teacher took his place on the pebble next to him. The three hundred students listened with fear and trembling to the beginning of the day's lecture. They knew they would be denied a day's food if they couldn't recite the main parts of the lecture to the teacher's aides responsible for hearing their recitation. Caterfly noticed that about forty aides were scattered throughout the crowd; their lot was mostly comprised of retired laborers and crippled soldiers.

When he had finished his introduction on the necessity of having a serious attitude, the enthusiastic instructor began the main section of his lesson.

His voice carried easily even to Caterfly who listened intently from the rear of the classroom.

"Work alone, my little friends—work *alone* justifies our existence here. Work, work, work. We ants have survived since the beginning of time because we have a proper view of life. We have survived all the dangerous predators of the garden because we labor incessantly not for ourselves but for our society—a society of eternal Antdom. We have survived and someday we will prevail over all the other creatures of the garden, because of our unbreakable unity. Small as we are, we are totally dedicated to the ideals of our society. Work is proof of our unity and dedication."

The teacher raised his voice and increased the tempo of the delivery of his lesson.

"Work for unity! Work for the ideals of Antdom! Work, work, work! Who am I? I am nothing! Who are you? You are nothing! We are nothing, but Antdom is something great and eternal! Antdom is everything! Don't worry about what you'll eat or how beautiful you look. Remember, you are nothing. Don't expect anything from Antdom. Ask from morning to night what you can sacrifice for Antdom."

Caterfly observed that the speaker's eyes seemed to glow and his antennae seemed to wave about more and more wildly as he spoke with increasing enthusiasm.

"My friends, Antdom is our home, our soiety, our existence. We must not permit any creature to destroy Antdom. If any creature, no matter how big or how small attacks our society in any way, we must fight to the bitter end—to the last mandible, leg, antenna. If any ant invades our territory, we must kill him! If he is more brown or less brown than we are, we must kill him for our own safety.

Work, work, work!
Kill, kill, kill!
Work, work, work!
Kill, kill, kill!

This is the secret of survival and success. Say it—shout it! Shout it!"
The crowd including Caterfly was quite taken by the exciting speech. The mesmerized audience began to shout in unison.   "Work, work, work!
Kill, kill, kill!
Work, work, work!
Kill, kill, kill!"

The teacher orator seemed quite pleased by the deafening chant. Immediately after the completion of the chant, a deathly silence fell upon the frenzied classroom.

The teacher concluded by saying, "My young friends, you are getting the right idea for survival and success. Before you go, don't forget to repeat the lesson to your assigned aide. Tomorrow, I'll teach you the virture of obedience."

Caterfly watched the lines form before each examiner. He had surprised himself by shouting violently with the crowd. He hadn't thought he was capable of such outbursts. He was both frightened and embarrassed, but he didn't know why.

The winged insect felt suffocated by the atmosphere of the classroom. Something inside him wanted to be free of the classroom and free of Antdom as well. Caterfly quietly backed out of the classroom while the ants were preoccupied by the recitation phase of the lesson. Once he felt sufficiently safe from the view of students and their supervisors alike, he turned and scurried away toward the mulberry tree. As he fled Antdom, he contemplated the next step of his journey.

He thought, "What I must do next frightens me, but what lays behind is even more frightening. I'd rather have hope in facing the unknown than to have no hope knowing what I face."

After ducking the sentries in their outposts and blazing his own paths to avoid well-used trails, he found himself within easy reach of the base of the mulberry tree by nightfall. An exhausted Caterfly made his bed in a clump of wild grass at the base of the tree that night.

CHAPTER 7

. . . in which he joins the Ant Army.

Sunrise found Caterfly shouting, "Black Jack, Black Jack" into the hole of the mulberry tree. He had made an important decision during the night and needed help.

A startled Black Jack peered out of the darkness of the small hole at Caterfly.

"Caterfly, you returned! You didn't forget me!" Black Jack exclaimed.

"Yes, I returned. I didn't forget, but I came to ask you for help."

"What do you need, my friend?" the black spider asked as he emerged into the morning's warmth.

"I want to fly!" Caterfly said excitedly.

"Fly?" Black Jack was taken aback by the wild remark.

"Yes, I want to go ballooning!"

"You? Ballooning, Caterfly?"

"Yes, ballooning."

"You seem to be a little too big or too old for such a thing, my friend. I had hoped that work would straighten you out and settle you down a bit, but you're crazier than ever!"

Caterfly was silent.

Black Jack, thinking that he had hurt him, apologized.

"I'm sorry, Caterfly, you woke me from a deep sleep. I'm a little cranky. You never really seemed crazy to me, just too idealistic. You never did seem very realistic according to the rules of nature. All creatures of nature know who they are and do some kind of work. You don't know who you are and you obviously aren't interested in work. Instead, you want to go ballooning and kill yourself."

Caterfly had been listening to his leggy black friend carefully. After a moment's pause, he spoke directly to Black Jack.

"I am myself, I am Caterfly. I know that much. I also know I like work, but for work in itself, not for any other purpose. I don't want to kill myself. I want to live. The light at the eastern end of the garden means hope and life to me. In that light I'll find myself and be truly alive. I must risk all to get there. I would die of old age trying to reach it on the ground struggling with the obstacles down there. Instead, I want to fly there like a bird. Hook me up to a giant filament so that a blast of air will carry me in that direction. Help me, Black Jack."

The spider listened intently, but he didn't like what he heard. He loved Caterfly as much as his brothers and he didn't want to see him risk his life in a wild adventure.

"On the other hand," he thought, "he must see an end to this illusion. He *has* to find himself someday. I prefer to live with a few illusions and not test them. Testing illusions is a dangerous process that can throw a creature out of balance with the order of nature, but Caterfly is no ordinary creature. Perhaps his wild gamble will lead him to some order he can understand and follow. I trust my instincts, and they serve me well; why shouldn't I let Caterfly follow his? If he has one chance in a hundred of reaching his goal, it must be worth the odds to him." After having carefully thought over the problem, the spider spoke again to Caterfly.

"Caterfly, I'll help you!"

"Good! When can we begin?"

"Now," Black Jack answered as he left the hole in the trunk and crawled a short distance out on the limb. There for a long while he remained motionless.

Caterfly observed his still friend for about twenty minutes and finally he crawled alongside him.

"Black Jack, I thought you said we could begin now?"

Without turning his head, the spider said, "Impatient Caterfly! How little you know about scientific things! I've been working on the ballooning project for twenty minutes already with my brain."

"I'm sorry," an embarrassed Caterfly said softly.

Black Jack thought aloud, "When the youngsters balloon, the filament that carries them is twenty times their length and one and a half times their width. You seem to be made of denser stuff than the young spiders. Therefore, the length of your flying cord will be twenty-five times your length and twice your width. More than twenty-five times your length might fold in a slack wind.

"Also, the silk cord will have to be specially designed to avoid sticking to every insect it encounters. I couldn't produce enough thread to make your huge flying apparatus on short notice. I'll make the frame with the help of my associates. Bits of very thin dry leaves and pieces of grass blow up here from the ground; you can help me paste them to the frame. I'll construct a harness to fit around your body.

"Your wings will give you an advantage over the spiders who balloon. You'll be able to execute slight turns—in the direction of the wind, of course. You'll have about fifteen percent control over your flight path. A little experimentation with your wings in flight will help.

"When you are close to your objective, you'll cut a

special thread which will release you and your harness. You will then turn end over end in the air for a few seconds, but your outstretched wings will help you drop gracefully, (hopefully) onto some tree leaves or, better still, into the pond itself. If you land in the pond, your harness will keep you afloat while you push at the water with your wings and make your way to land.

"The speed of the wind is critical in this undertaking. If you use a fast wind, you'll be more alert and less fatigued at the end of your journey: you'll have greater strength and judgment to make the proper maneuvers for a safe landing. However, if you make a mistake in a high wind, you would be blown far off course and probably be killed. A slow wind seems safer at first thought, but you'll get fatigued all those hours up there. You'll also be exposed that much longer to the killers of the air.

"You must decide what wind to ride. It's your life, Caterfly, so it's your choice.

Caterfly was silent throughout the spider's talk. He was amazed by the amount of thought Black Jack had already been doing on the project. After a little hesitation, he asked his friend a question that had been slowly forming in his insect mind.

"Do you want to ride the wind with me, Black Jack?"

"No, my friend," the answer came quickly.

"Some belong to the wind, Caterfly, and others to the water. Some creatures like myself belong to the earth. I love it and respect it, and in turn it takes care of me." After those words, Black Jack thought aloud again about the project. This time he went into greater detail as Caterfly listened appreciatively. Two black spiders resembling Black Jack joined the pair at sunset and lively discussions about the project continued until nightfall.

For three days, the team of spiders, captained by Black

Jack, worked continuously to construct the flying sail. Caterfly spent most of the time cutting dried leaves into strips for the spiders to paste on the sticky frame. The balloon resembled a large blade of grass which was suspended from its tip and base ends on parallel branches by a single silken cord. The spiders moved quickly and confidently through the length and breadth of their creation while they attached light materials to the threads until almost ninety percent of the area was covered. Black Jack had decided to leave ten percent of the area uncovered to reduce the stress of the wind on the surface by permitting a little wind to pass through the sail unobstructed by leaves or grass.

"After all, Caterfly, the young spiders go ballooning on a thread alone; we've given you a giant flying leaf to use!" Black Jack said as he tried the harness on Caterfly to test the fit.

"Tomorrow you fly, my friend. Get some sleep," he said without emotion in his voice.

Caterfly couldn't sleep. He watched his "balloon" flapping in the evening breeze. He also watched the light, the light at the far end of the garden as it seemed to beckon to him.

"Don't be afraid, Caterfly," it seemed to say. "Fear not the wind or the storms, the killers of the ground or the killers of the air. Come to me. Have courage and you will finally know yourself."

"Will that crazy thing really fly, or will it fall straight down?" Caterfly wondered. "Will I ever reach the light? Will a bird kill me on the way there or will a bat pick me off along with a hundred other insect snacks tomorrow night? Perhaps I'll be crushed to death or drown. Is the light only an illusion? Am I really a creature of the earth like Harry or Black Jack? Should I stay on earth like them and caress it and let it provide for me?"

The questions never ceased. Caterfly went without sleep. At sunrise, Black Jack crawled over to Caterfly and said, "The best time for you to leave is when the sun sets. That will minimize the dangers of birds and give you enough visibility to do some basic navigation during the first stage of your trip. You won't get too much activity on the part of the bats here for about three hours after the sun sets. If you pick the medium speed winds, you will be down after facing only two dangerous hours with the bats. In the darkness, you'll be able to see the light a lot better from up there. You should have enough moonlight tonight to make a safe landing. Most of the killers of the ground will be asleep when you land. Don't move around too much at night. Just find a safe place to sleep. Save your strength for travelling the last land distance to the light during the day. As I said, I would advise a medium speed at sunset. What do you think?"

Caterfly answered, "Black Jack, I don't know what I've done to deserve your friendship. You've made my wild desire a good possibility. You've tried to protect me from all possible dangers. Your science and logic are superb! I'll go along with the plan, or should I say, I'll let the plan take me away with it? Just promise me one thing." "What's that?" the spider responded.

"If you see me crushed to death or eaten by a bird, promise me that you won't blame yourself, since this is a journey I must take, and you've made it as safe as possible."

"I promise," the spider said with gentleness in his voice.

"Caterfly, you deserved my friendship from the moment you showed me you were good enough to trust me when I saved you from the birds. You trusted me and listened to me when the other smug insects ignored me and never bothered to see any good in me at all. Now you've witnessed that spiders aren't all bad and that we, too, have some intelligence. Now, Caterfly, you must promise me one thing."

"What's that, Black Jack?"

"If you make it, try to return to me one day and tell me about the light. Fair deal?"

"Fair deal, Black Jack!" Caterfly said joyfully. Once the exchange of promises was made, they shook many a leg in agreement.

At sunset, Black Jack placed the harness on the middle of Caterfly's body and locked it securely with threads from his body.

Caterfly could feel each wind vibrate through his sail and harness. The excitement was hard for him to bear. Caterfly's entire weight dangled from the harness and swayed a little with each breeze. One spider was stationed at the main supporting thread at the branch above waiting to cut the suspension line when Black Jack gave the command. Black Jack had stationed himself just below Caterfly and was prepared to cut the bottom support when Caterfly gave him the word.

After a tense ten-minute wait Caterfly decided upon a favorable wind. He was being hit by a series of medium to high velocity updrafts moving in an easterly direction.

"Now, Black Jack!" he shouted.

He heard the spider shout, "Now!" and the snap of the cut support line beneath him. He flew upward until he was almost even with the top support line when it too snapped. Caterfly, harness and kite, knifed wildly through the air turning end over end for the first few seconds.

The kite righted itself and he got his sense of balance. The wind seemed to be blowing incredibly fast, and when he looked groundward he was astonished. The trees were so far below they looked like wild clumps of grass. He could see the whole pond at one time; it was directly below him. He was above the setting sun; he could almost touch the clouds. Caterfly became elated over his vision of the garden. As Caterfly spun around in his harness, he made a joyful, but profound discovery. The world was bigger than his garden!

Below there seemed to be many gardens and hills a million times bigger than the hills in his tiny garden. Many shimmering ponds seemed to spin gracefully amidst new shades of orange, red, green, yellow, and brown. The light of the dying sun created a magic of its own.

All was well. The wind continued to blow away from the sun. Some disturbing thoughts began to trouble the tiny adventurer.

"There must be trillions of insects below," he thought. "What difference does it make if one of them—Caterfly—finds himself? What good will that do? One small insect is all that I am. My life cycle means nothing one way or the other to anything or any other creature. Why must I look for meaning or importance in my life? My only real use would be to help fill a bird's belly.

"Perhaps I would have been the greatest service in life working for the ants or being one good meal caught in Black Jack's web. They have a sense of purpose those rats, birds, spiders, and ants. Maybe my lack of meaning means that I should simply serve as food for creatures who know who they are and where they're going."

As Caterfly swirled through the evening sky at a breathtaking pace, he observed a flight of large birds halfway between himself and the treetops.

"Black Jack is brilliant!" he thought. "He made it possible for me to fly higher than the birds below, and I'm just an insect! He helped me just as Harry, the rat, did. They maybe despised creatures, but they were beautiful to me. What good could I do for them? None. What purpose do I have? None. The frog was right after all. Life is absurd. Look at me riding in a spider-made leaf and blowing away with the wind. How silly!

"The harder I try to find the truth, the more chances I take. The more chances I take, the sillier I become." Caterfly became gloomy as his self doubts harassed him. For some time he had been steadily facing the sun and watching it fade into the horizon. The twilight hour seemed to steep him in deep regrets about leaving his friends.

"What is Homer doing now? Where is Esmeralda?" he thought sadly. "Oh, why did I ever begin this journey?"

Just at that moment, his sail turned in the wind and Caterfly was wonderstruck by the radiance of the enormous light below. Tears formed in his eyes as he experienced the warmth and charm of the all-engulfing but soft radiance of the light. The light seemed to be pouring out of a great hole in a titanic hill. Slender shafts of the light seemed to penetrate even the furthest gardens. Caterfly bubbled over with joy as tears poured out of his insect eyes. The troublesome questions ceased. His mind was filled with one word only. Yes, yes, yes. Over and over the word repeated and filled his entire being. Yes, yes, yes. He felt no fear of the soft light filling him with peace and satisfaction. His only desire was to descend into the light below and lose himself there.

For the first time since the flight began, he manipulated his wings in the wind. He quickly discovered the proper angle to use his wings to create a slow descent into the light. For almost ten minutes, he had the sensation of descending slowly, but then a sudden updraft pushed him away from his goal. Since he was reaching the danger point of overshooting his goal, he snipped his harness release with his mouth and immediately plunged into an end over end free fall.

"Stretch your wings, Caterfly, stretch your wings," he thought in a panic as he remembered Black Jack's advice.

His stretched wings stabilized his descent. He no longer rolled wing over wing or fell end over end. The insect maintained a bumpy but long glide path toward the right side of the glowing white light that was growing larger and brighter every second.

"How beautiful!" Caterfly thought. "I wonder why all the birds in the world don't fly into the light and bask in it. What an experience!"

The light seemed to be calling to him to experience it to the fullest. "The moment of truth will come in a few seconds," he thought. "When I crash into the bottom of the light, I'll either die or solve the mystery of this beautiful glow. For the first time in my life, I feel I'm home."

Suddenly, a gust of wind turned Caterfly about. He found himself falling backwards for a few seconds and being blown further to the right of the light. Below him in the moonlight he could make out the tops of trees. As he tried to turn around and face the angle of descent, he spun end over as he crashed into the leaves of a tree. The harness took the shock of the initial impact, but it prevented Caterfly from getting a quick grip on the leaves as he glanced over them and fell from the tree. He had just enough time to stretch his wings to break his fall. He made half a somersault as he fell and landed with a tiny splash upside down in the water.

Caterfly panicked for a few seconds as he gulped water and couldn't breathe. After what seemed to him to be forever, he steadied his body in the water by stretching his wings and raising his head in order to breathe.

"I'm alive!" he thought gratefully.

He struggled in the dark water for about five minutes and finally managed to roll over by holding one wing close to his side and pushing on the water with the other. He took stock of the situation. Thanks to his harness, he floated easily. A few bats whizzed overhead. Crickets chirped everywhere. A few frogs called to one another.

"I won't drown now, but I'm fish bait for sure," he thought.

The wonderous light glowed with starlight radiance just to his left. "Maybe I didn't fail altogether," he thought. "Now my objective is to get to shore and find a safe place to sleep. I wonder if this is the same pond as the one where I started? No, the distance is too great."

He pushed at the water with his wings and propelled himself slowly to land. He thought of his encounter with Mr. Frog. He sang as he paddled. "Row, row, row your body, life is but a dream, row, row, row, your body, life is absurd . . . maybe!

"Yes, maybe, just maybe life has meaning after all," he thought hopefully.

It took him an hour to reach a section of the bank which was nearest to the light and another hour to climb the bank and find a suitable clump of grass. Restfully gazing at the wonderous light nearby and feeling deep satisfaction, an exhausted Caterfly fell into a deep sleep.

Chapter 8

. . . in which Caterfly learns a hard lesson and fights with former friends.

The warmth of the morning sun and the sound of frogs singing woke Caterfly. He felt refreshed from his deep sleep. After getting his bearings, he proceeded away from the pond in the direction of the source of light. Its radiance could be seen despite the daylight.

He had travelled uneventfully for about an hour ducking toads, snakes, and lizards as he moved through the undergrowth when suddenly he heard a familiar voice.

"Come on, come on, get moving my brothers, we want to move this food to the northern end of the pond by nightfall!"

"Bos, Bos," Caterfly cried out quite forgetting himself as he charged out of the high grass into a small bare spot where Bos and ten weary laborers were moving a dead earthworm.

"Caterfly, you!" Bos exclaimed. "How in the world did you get here? What in the world are you doing here?"

Caterfly quickly explained his flight and his purpose for seeking the great light, skipping the part about running away from the ant community.

Bos ant seemed angry.

"Caterfly, the way I understand it, you deserted Ant-dom and your duties."

Caterfly was beginning to feel sorry he had been so friendly to his old boss.

"You will work with us, Caterfly. You will help us move this food supply to its destination. Let's go!"

"No!" Caterfly said sharply and without hesitation.

"Listen, Caterfly, I don't owe you an explanation, but I'll give you one for old times' sake," Bos said angrily. "There is a war going on between various tribes of brown ants and red ants. After days of forced march, our fourth army arrived here, the furthest outpost. We form the eastern defense line. We are under orders to harass the red ant tribes in this area and to keep them off balance so they can't mount a major offensive on key brown ant tribes in this area. We have committed 30,000 ant soldiers for this task and they must eat! I've given you reason to help us, since you like to be satisfied by reasons for things. Come, join us. There is much work to do!"

"No!" Caterfly said firmly.

"Caterfly, listen to me," Bos said as he tried to suppress his startled state of mind. "The ten ants here are hardened killers. They are under my orders as I am under orders. You must either labor with us for the rest of your days or die here and serve as a food supply." "You listen," Caterfly said angrily. "I will not be a slave! I have my own purposes for my life. I didn't travel such great distances and endure such hardships and face such dangers to be stopped by you!"

"Caterfly, wake up!" Bos shouted. "Look at what you face. We are professional killers; we will kill you without hesitation. Are you prepared to kill? Is it in you to kill?"

Caterfly studied the group of brown ants and saw the evidence of hard fighting in their faces and bodies. A few of the ants had lost a leg or an antenna. Two ants had lost an eye each. All of the ants including Bos had horrible scars on their bodies.

"This is going to be real bad," Caterfly thought.

He studied the lay of the land. He couldn't outrun the ants in the dense undergrowth. He would have to stand and fight. But where? Behind the ants lay a muddy puddle of water. Although he didn't relish the possibility of drowning, he considered rushing the ants and pushing some of them into the puddle to discourage them. Caterfly was scared. Images of the horrible death of the young frog buried under a pile of killers while it thrashed about helplessly frightened him. He wanted to run, but he knew that that would only encourage the killers.

"They have no right to kill me or enslave me," he thought sternly as the ants formed a half-circle and prepared to rush him all at the same time.

Without any signal that he could see, the ants began to run at Caterfly. Before they could close the gap, Caterfly charged at the center of the semicircle. Only one ant was trampled under him, but the others moved aside and Caterfly found himself facing the brink of the puddle. Not one ant had panicked or had been pushed into the water. Disappointed, Caterfly wheeled about to face his enemy. The ants had quickly reorganized. Even the one that had been run over limped alongside his companions as a newly formed semicircle closed in on Caterfly.

Since the water blocked any possible retreat on his

part, Caterfly had to meet his enemy head on. As the semicircle moved in for the kill, he directed his remarks to the leader. "Listen to me, Bos. You've killed a hundred insects, but I've killed a hundred false ideas. You are professionals, but so am I. You want to continue your lives and so do I. You will fight for your way of life and so will I. Bos, you are responsible for what happens to these ants. You'll be responsible for what happens to them if you attack me. I'll do whatever I have to do to be free."

"Attack!" was the sharp response from Bos.

The first ant to charge Caterfly was unexpectedly struck by a backward stroke of the winged insect's left wing. The ant was catapulted into the middle of the pond. It took all his energy just to try to keep his head above water and not drown. The second ant that confronted him was hit squarely on his head with the front edge of Caterfly's wing. The blow was so severe it incapacitated him for the remainder of the fight.

Six ants ducked under his flailing wings at almost the same instant that the first two casualties occurred. They immediately fastened themselves to various parts of his body and prepared to cut through wing and leg alike.

Caterfly began twisting and turning in an attempt to shake off his opponents. As he twisted in frustration, he noticed two ants had not yet joined the battle. Standing a few inches away, Bos and a large tough-looking brown ant calmly assessed the battle.

"They are waiting for the right moment to deal a fatal blow to me," Caterfly thought with anger rising. "Bos probably sacrificed the first two ants to gain that split second his group needed to get under my wings and fasten themselves to me. What an excellent military leader Bos is—so sure of himself—so clever when it comes to killing helpless insects!"

Caterfly twisted his body and turned in circles, but could not shake off his tormentors. The blue and white striped insect shuddered as pain erupted from his hind legs and wings.

In an instant, Caterfly found himself off balance, but as he tried to regain his balance, he was shocked by the sight and frenzy of the ants clinging to his legs. Shock gave way to reaction as he turned on the ant that was attached to his left foreleg. Without hesitation, he snipped him in two.

"So you would cripple Caterfly," he shouted. The shock of his wound and the ensuing pain incapacitated the ant for the duration of the battle.

Caterfly began to feel severe pains as the biting through the base of his wings continued. The pain cleared his head. He grew calm; he stopped turning and thrashing.

"Bos and the other one will come in to finish me off when they think I'm too tired or hurt to put up strong resistance," he thought. "What would happen if Bos himself was surprised and injured as he moved in? Maybe the others would lose heart and retreat."

Caterfly flopped on the ground and gave no resistance to those who were attempting to sever various parts of his body with ant precision. He had one bad moment when he thought that he might be severed into sections before Bos would join the battle. After that moment, which seemed longer and more painful than all the moments of his life, Bos and his partner ran at Caterfly's head. As they neared, Caterfly leapt to his feet and charged at Bos. Bos was unable to turn away in time. Caterfly grabbed one of his front legs and neatly snipped it off. As Bos rolled over in pain, his henchman fastened himself to Caterfly's right antenna. Desperately, Caterfly butted his head into his new attacker, crushing and trying to dislodge the large brown antagonist. The hind quarters stopped moving, but the remainder of the tough ant somehow remained fastened to the antenna. Desperately, Caterfly butted his right antenna—with the killer ant still attached—to the ground, but he couldn't shake off any of his opponents no matter how he tried.

As Caterfly tried to dislodge the tenacious ant on his antenna, Bos managed to attach himself to Caterfly's neck. In great panic, Caterfly thrashed about crazily in a desperate attempt to get rid of his persecutors. His body was racked with pain. The tormentor on his head abandoned his work on the damaged antenna and shifted his attention to his victim's right eye. His wings were causing him intense pain; he knew in a minute that they too would be lost. His plight seemed hopeless; Bos was beginning the process of decapitation.

The powerful primitive instinct of survival surfaced, a tidal wave of anger unleashed in Caterfly. Instead of submitting to his fate, he swelled with the power of rage. In one final angry attempt to free himself from his tormentors, he rushed directly up a small mound and leaped into the puddle. He was submerged for a few seconds by the force of the dive. The momentum also carried the winged insect and his riders to the center of the puddle where the first ant Caterfly thrust into the water was still struggling to stay afloat.

The ants relinquished their death grips on Caterfly in exchange for holds that would keep their heads out of water. In failing to do this, two of them drowned in the process.

Bos was bobbing alongside Caterfly holding on to the front edge of his right wing. His voice betrayed his fear and confusion as he said excitedly, "Caterfly, you're crazy! How could you do such a thing! We're all going to drown!"

Caterfly turned his head and looked at him gravely with his uninjured left eye. "How could *I* do such a thing?" he replied calmly.

Caterfly appraised the situation. He had suffered terrible punishment, but he was not mortally wounded. He felt pain, but he could bear it. Caterfly was still afloat barely, but he doubted if he could propel himself ashore due to the damage to his wings. But now he knew that he wouldn't drown.

"Unless these ants have a change of attitude, they'll kill me once I manage to get to shore," he thought. "No sense even trying to make dry land if the thought of killing me is still in their brains."

Disregarding their screams of panic, Caterfly began to roll his body from side to side in the water. Since most of his body was underwater at any given time, the ants found themselves plunged underwater time and time again. The drowning sensation demoralized them completely. After a few minutes, Caterfly stretched his throbbing and tattered wings and used them to stabilize his battered body. The ants that had fallen into the water with him were joined by the earliest battle victim.

They held desperately to the body and wings of Caterfly. They realized that their lives were at the mercy of the insect they so mercilessly tried to kill.

"I'm sorry," Caterfly laughed sarcastically, "but you damaged my body and wings so much that I have trouble remaining stable in the water. As a matter of fact, we might all find ourselves on the bottom if I can't hold things together here. What would you suggest, Bos?"

Bos answered in a deeply troubled voice, "Caterfly, for your sake, please take us to the shore."

"For my sake, Bos?" Caterfly asked with mock laughter in his voice. "That's not a good enough reason, is it? Remember—to you and our little group here I have no value. I'm just food or a slave, right? I have no reason to save myself, especially after already being nearly killed by you, do I? Well, do I?"

Bos detected anger under Caterfly's feigned laughter. He was as frightened as any member of his ant troop. "An angry Caterfly that had no reason to live would have nothing to lose if he plunged us all to the bottom," he thought. "How can we carry out our mission to gather food if we are all dead, and for no good reason? How stupid I was to attack Caterfly!"

"Caterfly," he said aloud, "I am deeply sorry I gave the order to attack you. I ask you, for the sake of the kingdom of the brown ants you once served so well, to take us to shore. Once on shore, we'll take the worm to our troops and you'll go free."

"You make a little sense, Bos," Caterfly said sharply. "You, of course, mean that we will part company in peace once we reach land. I do not intend to help you carry the worm anywhere."

"Yes, that's what I meant," Bos said in a relieved tone.

"Your reason for a truce does not suit me," Caterfly responded. "All of you get off my body!" he shouted.

The frightened ants began to plead for mercy.

Bos shouted above the crowd, "We'll drown, Caterfly. You can't do this, we have a right to live just as you have a right to live!"

"Quiet, let Bos talk," commanded Caterfly.

The ants fell silent instantly.

Bos stumbled through his words, "We have no right to cling to Caterfly or use him as a raft. He has the right to be free of us in every way. He does not have to cooperate with us in any way. We owe our lives to Caterfly . . . I hope he will find some reason to take us to dry land. Duty is our reason to live, but I understand now that duty does not have to be his reason to live."

Caterfly was impressed, but he still wasn't satisfied. "Bos, are you afraid of failing in your duty more than you fear death itself?"

"Yes," Bos said gravely.

"Then you will fulfill a condition for the survival of your troop," Caterfly responded.

"Yes, anything, Caterfly."

"I'll try to save these members of your group if you are willing to forfeit your life here and now!" Caterfly said sharply.

Bos was totally surprised by the request. "It is better that I drown and my command survive to find another captain," Bos said firmly. "If you wish, I'll let go of your wing and that will seal the truce. Tell me when you want me to let go."

Caterfly eyed the dedicated soldier; his anger gave way to the pity he felt for Bos.

"You really mean what you say, don't you Captain Bos?" Caterfly asked in a serious tone.

"Yes, I do, Caterfly. I am true to my word; I carry out my duties faithfully."

Caterfly wasn't satisfied with his answer. For a long time, he floated silently and easily on the water while the ants grew weak and tired clinging to him.

Bos broke the silence. "Caterfly, soon we'll drown. Why don't you try to take us to shore?"

Caterfly answered softly, "Bos, I'm not responsible if you ants drown. You should never have attacked me, besides something is still not straight in my mind."

"What is that, Caterfly?"

"What was your duty, the one you had to carry out?"

"My duty was and is to bring food to the fighting ants. My immediate duty was to carry the worm to the north end of the pond. You were a target of opportunity, Caterfly; a food target. I decided to take you too."

"So," Caterfly said grimly, "I'm a target of opportunity. My life and my hopes just happened to get in the way of your military priorities at the wrong time. Was it your duty to carry a dead worm or have your entire command destroyed by a target of opportunity?"

"I made a tactical blunder, Caterfly, I know that. Now, I interpret my duty as getting my battered group and the worm to the objective."

"What about me?" Caterfly said as he eyed him cautiously.

"Once we arrive on land, you will be free to go as you please," Bos said directly.

"What is my guarantee of safety?" Caterfly answered. "Don't give me any double talk, military terms or promises; put it in words I can accept," Caterfly said directly.

Bos did not speak for several long minutes. Finally he looked at Caterfly and said, "Caterfly, my group is not in very good condition to fight you again. If we sustain any more injuries, we won't have the strength to carry the worm back to camp. If we managed to kill you, at our present strength, we could not carry both you and the worm back to our camp. By the time we sent for help, the red ants might attack us and make a prize of both you and the worm. We have lost too much time as it is; I must minimize the dangers to my command. It would now be in our best interests to let you go free."

Caterfly was satisfied by his answer. He pulled painfully with both his wings and moved slowly toward the edge of the puddle. After a few minutes, the ants slowly crawled off of Caterfly and made their way toward dry land. Caterfly weakly pulled himself on to the shore.

As he crawled into a clump of grass near the edge of the puddle, he watched Bos and his command slowly push and drag the worm into the tall grass. Bos took just one backward glance at Caterfly and shouted, "I used to like you, Caterfly, when you knew your place, but now I fear you because I don't know what you're becoming."

"I'm alive at least," he thought weakly. "They didn't kill me, but unfortunately they had losses." A tear formed in his one good eye. His body was racked with fatigue and dull pain from his wounds.

"I only wanted to find the answers to my questions about myself; why did they force me to be such a vicious creature? Why?" He fell into a deep sleep just before night fell.

All during the next day Caterfly did not move from his resting place. He neither ate nor drank that day. He slept a great deal and sometimes tensely watched small groups of red ants running wildly on the ground nearby.

At night, he gazed at the immensely bright light nearby for inspiration. "Old radiant light," he whispered. "I believe in you; I hope you believe in me. I came to you; I hope you truly led me as I believe you have. I'm sorry I don't know your name if you have one, but I believe you are goodness and peace itself. The closer I come to you, the brighter you shine outside of me. The closer I come to you, the brighter you shine inside of me. Now I'm battered, bruised, exhausted, and older than when I started, but when I see you shine so brightly, those things don't matter. The trip was worth it because you are worth it. Please let me come closer still and find the answers I seek before I die. Somehow I know the answers are in you. Please help me because I can't make it alone." Caterfly fell comfortably asleep in the light.

Chapter 9

. . . in which he listens (bewildered) to philosophers.

Upon awakening, Caterfly looked about for possible antagonists and then cautiously slipped out of the clump of grass. He limped as quickly as his battered body would carry him through an open area between patches of high grass. After clearing the grass obstacle, he laboriously and painfully crawled up a mild incline for over four hours.

Again and again he fought the temptation to stop as fatigue and pain tested his determination. At the end of four heroic hours, he fainted from weakness. When he awoke an hour later, he continued his climb.

"There can be no turning back now," he thought determinedly, "I must go on or die trying!"

As he continued through the long moments of struggle, he felt a strange numbness overtaking him. His head cleared and his tired eyes fixed themselves on two figures emerging from underneath a big brown leaf on the path.

"Wasps!" he gasped.

The two much respected but deadly insects approached Caterfly. Caterfly did not flinch. He stared steadily at them with his good eye but he remained silent.

To his astonishment, the wasp nearest to him spoke in a sweet voice.

"Stranger, your wounds and general condition tell us that you have bravely overcome all obstacles to come to the Hill of Seekers. We welcome you. My brother and I are guards at this entrance way. We will not harm you, instead we will bring you to others in our group who will help you. I am Marc and this is my brother Max."

"I am Caterfly," the insect said weakly only half believing what Marc said. "I'm happy to meet you both; I would appreciate your help, but I'm not as weak as I look," he said defensively.

Without further discussion, the wasps edged under Caterfly and carried him higher up the hill on their backs. After a few minutes, they stopped and removed themselves as they gently let Caterfly come to rest on the ground. They flew past him to return to their posts.

Caterfly soon found himself surrounded by a small group of insects. A large black ant told him not to worry about anything, since the group was dedicated to helping others. Caterfly wanted to ask many questions, but he was too tired to open his mouth. His eyes filled with the tears of gratitude as ants, crickets, termites, and a grasshopper dashed about his body applying various soothing balms to his many wounds.

A praying mantis, called Kim by her companions, fed him bits of delicious cherry leaf and gave him a few sips of water from a tiny seed shell as the others went quietly about their doctoring. In response to such concern and gentleness, Caterfly fell into a deep and peaceful sleep.

He awoke amidst the quiet chattering of his newly found benefactors. The black ant faced him and spoke calmly but directly to him. "Caterfly, you probably feel much better this morning. Your wings will be healed completely in a few days. You'll soon regain all of the sight in your right eye. I don't know much about your species, but your legs will probably be completely healed in a few days. You are welcome to stay here with us the rest of your days if you choose. But before you do anything at the Hill of Seekers, you should report to the acceptance committee a little farther up the hill."

"Gentle healers," Caterfly said gratefully, "you have been so very kind to me—a stranger. Your group is the most loving group of insects I've encountered in my short life, and I'd love to join you. You understand, I hope, that as long as I feel that I must find myself, I wouldn't be of much service to any group. I beg you to remember me as a grateful insect, because grateful I am. I must go on my way. But I will speak to the council. Thank you."

The group of kindly mendicants cheered Caterfly on his way as he moved briskly in the direction pointed out by the black ant.

Before very long, he encountered a hummingbird, an earthworm, and a small green turtle.

Caterfly felt a little nervous in their presence. There was great dignity and gravity in their bearing. For long moments, no one spoke. The trio scrutinized him with all their senses.

The very strong, high pitched voice of the worm startled Caterfly. "Young stranger, why did you come to the Hill of the Seekers?"

The blue and white striped insect relaxed, since the question seemed an ordinary one for a committee member to ask a stranger.

He calmly answered, "My name is Caterfly. I come from far away seeking answers about myself and life."

The trio seemed to nod in unison.

"These are not my enemies," Caterfly thought. "I'll just be myself, I'll relax."

The hummingbird asked the second question. "Caterfly, what made you feel you could find answers here?"

Caterfly calmly directed his remark to all questions. "I feel that the light coming from this hill is the truth and therefore all my questions will be answered and all my problems will be solved."

For a moment, the trio gathered in a huddle and then turned once again to face the adventurer.

The turtle spoke to Caterfly in a very deep voice, "You are still very, very, young. Why don't you enjoy life now and postpone the pursuit of truth until you are older?"

Caterfly thought for a moment and then answered, "Because I cannot arrive at the fullest enjoyment of my life until I find the answers I need about myself and the world."

The trio remained silent for awhile, but their eyes never left the winged insect.

The turtle spoke again in his deep voice, "Most of the insects who come here leave empty and discouraged. There are no easy answers from what we can see. We want you to know that. We are just an acceptance committee; we can make no guarantee what you will discover here. Do you understand, Caterfly?"

"Yes, I understand," Caterfly said quietly as he tried to hide his disappointment. "I would appreciate the opportunity to seek truth on the Hill of the Seekers."

The trio drew into a second huddle. In a moment they moved out of the huddle and faced Caterfly once again.

The worm addressed Caterfly in his high pitched voice, "Welcome to the Hill of the Seekers, Caterfly. May you find yourself and the answers you seek about life here!"

At that moment, the three companions embraced him and gave him a little advice on how to find his way about the hill.

He soon learned that the Hill had two major areas of activity: the area of the philosophers and the area of the religious. Other smaller groups of insects were scattered about the Hill. As he crawled briskly toward the philosophers, he passed a few solitary insects who preferred to be alone on their search for answers.

As he made his way through a dusty space of ground littered with dead leaves, he was almost deafened by a loud uproar coming from the other side of a huge rock which obstructed the path he was travelling. As he rounded the rock, he looked with disbelief upon the philosopher's community. There before him a hundred insects of various types were milling about singly or in large groups and shouting their ideas at the top of their insect voices. Caterfly crawled into a clump of weeds overlooking the grounds and watched the activities of the philosophers with utter fascination.

"You're Caterfly?" A kindly voice turned Caterfly's head to the left where he saw a dark brown grasshopper edging toward him.

"Yes, I am," he answered.

"I learned your name from the council. I'm sorry I'm late. I was supposed to show you around the philosopher's camp. I can see you're upset by all the shouting, but after awhile you'll find yourself doing the same thing to make your point."

"Make my point?" Caterfly asked.

"Yes, all philosophers try to make their point about life, death, immortality, mortality, ethics, nature, the origins of the gardens and so on and so forth. You'll enjoy it after awhile. It's just like playing a game, you know."

Caterfly was puzzled. He said, "I'm not here to prove a point. I'm here to learn the truth about myself and the world."

"Yes, I understand," the grasshopper said knowingly, "but is it truth if half the insects in the world have other ideas? You must prove your truth to others by logic or force of will. That's what it's all about."

"That's what it's all about, is it?" Caterfly thought. "It seems that I've heard that remark before." He remained silent, he was obviously confused and disappointed.

"Look, Caterfly, you'll make out alright here. You seem fairly smart. All you need to do is follow the proper method of becoming a good philosopher. First, for your initiation, you must hear a summary of the four dominant philosophies here. Then you'll learn some terms like existence, essence, fate, free will, causality, unmoved mover, *a priori*, God, monad, universal and so on. Then you'll learn to use logic to present your theories to others. Once you're ready, you'll learn to debate, to defend your theories from attack. You'll also soon learn how to slash and destroy the theories of others. After some verbal warfare, if you're lucky, the other philosophers will pay more attention to you. Who knows, in time you might develop a big enough following, your group will be able to shout down other groups. At that point, your truth will gain validity. You will be right; your truth will prevail! Exciting prospect, isn't it?"

Caterfly nodded his head to humor his adviser. "Philosophy must be more than this," he thought.

He turned his head away from the grasshopper for a moment and viewed the seemingly crazed group of insects below. Some were having one-to-one confrontations, some seemed to discuss things more quietly in small groups but turned into one loud vocal unit while engaging other groups that didn't share their views. Still others were milling about and shouting at every passer-by.

"It would take me more than one lifetime to learn anything about myself here," Caterfly thought.

"Mr. Grasshopper, would you please tell me a little about the main trends of thought here?" Caterfly asked politely.

"Call me Bert, Caterfly," he responded. "You could learn the trends at initiation, you know."

"Yes, Bert, but I'd appreciate some idea before I decide to go through with the process," Caterfly answered.

"The process?" Bert asked.

"Yes Bert, the process of trying to find truth through thinking," Caterfly said.

"Thinking is the only way to find truth. You talk as though you believe alternatives exist!" The grasshopper said in disbelief.

"Bert, I'm a little confused. Would you tell me about some of the basic concepts being present here?" Caterfly asked as he tried to duck an unnecessary argument.

"O.K., but I'll be very brief," Bert said as he began to lose interest in Caterfly due to his seeming wavering faith in philosophy.

"Some believe the world, including the gardens, all creatures, the sun, the moon, the stars — that the world is just an accident. Pieces of matter like apples were flying through space and they smashed together — and whamo! A world was created. The purpose of all creatures is to make order and purpose out of confusion. We must put meanings on things because nothing has a meaning. Life, therefore, has as much meaning as we put on it — no more.

"A second trend only varies a bit from the one I mentioned. The insects in that school of thought hold that the world started the same way I mentioned, but we can never add meaning because confusion and disorder are everywhere including in our minds. They say the best we can do is to enjoy the confusion itself. Doing this, we'll be happy, because unhappiness is caused by creatures looking for order where none exists. This group, of course, feels that logic itself is impossible and there is no such thing as reason in creatures. They feel that our minds are out of control at all times and even the study of logic won't make us reasonable. They believe that we can do whatever we want to do without blame, since we can't be judged for our actions, because everything and everyone is out of control anyway."

Caterfly listened silently and tried to absorb as much as he could from Bert.

"The third group also believes in the accident theory of creation. They feel that once the accident took place, however, everything settled down in good order. They feel that the world, the stars, and the moon are part of a big machine. Everything is part of a big machine, including us. We are little machines. We act according to the rules of our individual nature. I hop about, you crawl and fly, a bird walks and flies. We can only do what our nature orders us to do, nothing more. Each nature is in its own order. There is no confusion at all if we follow the strong impulses of our own nature. Society should have order and everyone has a definite part to play in his own group."

Caterfly listened intently. He wanted to tell the grasshopper that he couldn't fly and that he had no group, but Bert was intent on finishing his summary.

"The other major group feels that the world was created out of nothing. They believe in a god idea. Some of them believe that the Creator of the universe cares about his creation. Others in that group feel that the Creator is indifferent toward his creation. Those who maintain a caring Creator go join the religious group sooner or later. Those who believe that the Creator is uncaring spend their days here trying to determine why he doesn't care and how we can think our way back to the source of all thought. This group looks for reasons and order in everything. This group, whether or not they believe in a caring or uncaring creator, seems unified in as much as they feel there is something that each creature has in common with his maker and that thing is immortality. Are you satisfied, Caterfly?"

"Yes," Caterfly answered. "You were very kind to give me all that information. I need a day to think over what I will do."

"Well, I hope you join us in your search for truth, Caterfly. I gave you some basics. There are other philosophies here, mind you. There is enough here to keep you flying about the rest of your life."

"Bert, not that it means anything, but I want you to know I can't fly!" Caterfly said with no real purpose in mind except to clear away the mistake.

"Caterfly, don't tell me you can't fly. Peggy can fly and she is a member of your species!" Bert said emphatically.

"Peggy?" Caterfly said in a startled voice.

"Yes, Peggy! Look over there!" Bert pointed with his antenna to a small group of arguing insects just to the left of a large group of birds and rats.

Caterfly was stunned and delighted by the sight of another creature who looked exactly like himself! He lost control of himself and shouted at the top of his voice, "I'm not alone in the world, I'm not a freak! I'm not alone!"

Chapter 10

. . . in which Caterfly finds another like himself!

"Peggy, Peggy!" Caterfly shouted into the crowd of shouting philosophers.

Caterfly was awe struck as Peggy turned her head in his direction and flew toward him!

"This is impossible, but she's flying!" he thought. "She's the most beautiful creature I've ever seen."

Caterfly leaped out of the clump of grass in order to be near her when she landed. Within seconds Peggy fluttered down in a position facing Caterfly.

The two blue and white striped insects stared at each other in silence.

Bert broke the silence, "Caterfly this is Peggy, Peggy meet Caterfly."

The insects nodded.

Bert spoke again. "You see, Caterfly, you just proved my point. Truth cannot exist alone. You have to see yourself or your views in another to give those views validity. When you were alone you were unhappy, but now that you met a creature like yourself, you will find new meaning and strength in just being Caterfly."

Caterfly only paid half attention to Bert; he was captivated by Peggy.

Peggy broke the silence, her sweet voice sounded musical to Caterfly. "What is your first name?"

"They just call me Caterfly," he said.

"They used to call me Caterfly and Butterpillar too," she said jokingly. "It's not important what name they give you, but what you call yourself and what you think of yourself."

"Did you name yourself Peggy?"

"Yes, of course."

"It's the most beautiful name I've ever heard," he said softly.

"Why, thank you Caterfly."

"Are there more of us, Peggy?"

"I met one other, a male like yourself. He was better looking than you," she said. She quickly added, "not that looks mean anything. His thinking was untogether and he left the philosophers to return to his garden."

"I guess you miss him," Caterfly said awkwardly.

"Not especially," she said. "I don't seek any comfort from my own kind although it would be nice to have an enduring relationship with one of my own kind." She stared deeply into Caterfly's good eye and also into his wounded eye which seemed to be healing.

Caterfly was thrown off guard by her directness. He remained still. Bert lost interest in their conversation and hopped away.

"Are you a warrior, Caterfly?" she asked fearfully.

"I realize there are many scars on my body, Peggy, but I received them trying to protect myself from attack on my life."

"I can understand that," she said with a sigh of relief. "I hate violence of any kind to any creature, don't you?"

"Yes, Peggy. I hate violence and I hate myself for the violence I did to the ants who attacked me."

"That's good," she responded, "but you shouldn't hate yourself. Just hate the situations in the world that bring the worst out of all of us at times. If it were necessary, would you defend me from an attack on my life?"

"Yes, I would, Peggy, to the best of my ability," Caterfly said bravely.

Peggy smiled warmly. "Would you ever do violence to me even if you grew angry with me?"

"No! I could never harm you! How could I harm the most beautiful creature I've ever seen in my life!" Caterfly said emphatically.

Again, Peggy smiled warmly. "Caterfly, you said you would defend my life. Would you defend my ideas from attack?"

Caterfly almost said yes, but he hesitated.

"Suppose her ideas are wrong according to my way of thinking," he mused. "Should I agree with her ideas just to please her? If I do that then why didn't I just go along with Esmeralda in the first place? I better be careful how I answer."

"Well?" she asked directly.

"I'm sure your ideas are good and if I agreed with them I'd help you to defend them from attack," he said with sincerity ringing in his voice.

"If you agreed?" she said abruptly. "You have a typical male's view of a female, Caterfly! It's not really important to me that you think I'm beautiful or that you would defend my person from attack. My ideas are more important to me! My ideas are my life. Any male here would probably rush to save the life of a female of his species, but it takes a rare male to save the life of his female's ideas! Frankly, I'm disappointed although I really shouldn't have expected anything else."

Caterfly felt crushed by her remarks.

"She's still smiling," he thought. "At least she isn't angry. I just don't understand her."

He looked at her directly and said, "I'm not much of a

philosopher, Peggy. I've had no training, but I'd appreciate it if you gave me the basic idea of your beliefs."

"Yes, gladly," she said. "Basically, I believe in a world that was created by intelligence. The intelligence or Intelligent One will forever remain unknown because it is impossible for our finite minds to comprehend the infinite. The intelligence in the universe is eternal and boundless. We have no way of coping with these concepts. The best thing we can do as philosophers is to forget the boundless eternal forces and the cause of how we got here. We should concentrate on how we could all get along together in our gardens despite our species and despite our instincts which appear to conflict at times. We should accept our fate that we can never solve the unknowns in life. We should accept the fact that we only have a few days on this earth and try to live those days in harmony and peace."

"Your philosophy is beautiful, Peggy," Caterfly said after thinking a moment.

"That's the nicest compliment I ever received, Caterfly. You are most kind," she said joyfully. "Do you agree with me?"

"Let me think for awhile, Peggy, and don't be upset if I have some reservations O.K.?"

Peggy seemed pleased.

"Caterfly, I'm used to others not agreeing with me. You take time and think. How much time do you need? My friends over there need me; I should go soon. Philosophy is my life you know."

"Peggy, stay awhile," Caterfly said. "I'm going to challenge you to do something very difficult."

"I like challenges," she said. "Go ahead."

"I challenge you to stay by me for one day, but under the condition that neither of us say one word to the other!"

Peggy was surprised by the challenge. "One day is a long time, Caterfly. What would we do—crawl about together, climb a tree, fly over the philosophers a few times to irritate them or what?"

"Peggy, it's up to you. I'll do anything you like, but I'm afraid I can't fly," Caterfly responded as he wondered how his handicap would affect Peggy.

"Nonsense!" she said laughingly. "You think you can't fly, but you can. Once you get that negative word out of your thinking, you'll fly. I know our wings are too short for our bodies, I know our bodies are too heavy in relationship to our wings, but we can fly, Caterfly. We can fly! I can fly; you can fly too! I accept your challenge. We will spend a day in silence, but in that day I'll show you how to fly. Agreed?"

Caterfly wanted to explain his early failures at flight to her, but he felt she was so positive that there was no sense arguing with her. He longed for a day with her and he was willing to withstand the embarrassment of falling tail over head in attempted flights.

"Agreed!" he said happily.

Chapter 11

. . . wherein he learns to fly!

In the five hours that preceded sunset, Peggy gave Caterfly flying lessons. After several spectacular and embarrassing spills, he learned to arch his upper back and turn the front edge of his wings downward as he ran forward. Amidst the almost constant smiles and laughter of his companion, he finally found himself airborne for a few seconds.

"I'd rather crawl," he thought. "I'm using muscles I've never used before and how they hurt. I'm tired all over and Peggy is still very fresh looking. She seems to have so much patience with me. She looks so beautiful. I wish I could do something to show her how much I appreciate her."

As he was thinking, Peggy smiled and motioned to him to follow her up the stem of a large plant. They established themselves side by side on a firm leaf that pointed directly into the sunset. The insect companions watched the orange orb throw its last rays into the approaching darkness.

Caterfly mustered the courage to cover Peggy's back with his right wing. She turned toward him slowly and gave him a warm and appreciated look. She thus fell asleep under the protection of his wing. Caterfly watched the play of the fireflies and the movement of the moon and stars as imperceptible as those movements were to less observing creatures. He could not sleep despite the charm of the night. Something was missing. He gently removed his wing from his companion's back and turned completely around on the leaf. An ocean of soft white light flooded his good eye.

"Beautiful, just beautiful," he whispered to the light as tears formed in both eyes. He opened his wounded eye a little and the friendly light flowed through it with a healing warmth. He glanced at the leaf beneath his feet but soon discovered that he could only see it with his left eye.

"This charming light is different than the light of the sun or of fireflies," he thought. "This beautiful light grows brighter as I move toward it. It grows brighter outside of me and inside of me as I move closer and closer to it. What does this mean?

"Why don't all the creatures see it? Why don't the philosophers, as close as they are to it with their camp, take more interest in it?"

Caterfly closed his eyes and bathed himself in the friendly all pervading glow. He fell asleep in peace and contentment.

He was awakened abruptly at the first rays of the morning sun by a few tugs on his good antenna. He awoke to find himself looking at the puzzled expression on Peggy's face. Since she intended to honor the non-talking agreement until noontime arrived, she could only use the expression of her face to ask Caterfly why he turned away from her during the night.

Caterfly sensed what she wanted to know, but did not want to break the pact either. He simply displayed his warmest smile to indicate that nothing was wrong.

Peggy returned the smile to signal that her question would keep until noon.

Again, the flying lessons began in earnest. After an hour's silent review of back bending and wing tilting techniques, Peggy led her student to a gentle slope just to the west of the philosopher's camp. She ran a few steps down the hill, threw her head back, curved her wings forward and took off.

"I must hold my head high," Caterfly thought as he followed suit. He raced forward as fast as he was able. He threw his head back, curved his wings forward and beat them rapidly.

After a doubtful second, he left the ground. His wings fluttered in the warm gentle breeze. Exhilarating seconds lapsed before he dared to think, "I'm flying! It's impossible, but I'm actually flying on my own wing power!"

Caterfly felt uncomfortable in this new position—head back, wing-tip down. But he was too excited by his first true flight to be overly concerned. More seconds passed as Peggy maneuvered and flew directly in front of her matching blue and white striped friend. She flew slowly in a straight line to make it easy for Caterfly to follow.

After being airborne just half a minute, Caterfly grew anxious because he could no longer see flowers, weeds, or bushes on either side of him. He craned his neck to look down, but he fell immediately into a frightening nosedive. Below he could see the flowers, weeds, bushes, and ground rushing up at him!

He frantically threw his head back and fluttered his wings as madly as he could. He crashed sideways into a tall clump of crabgrass which broke his fall before he hit the ground.

It took a few seconds for Peggy to realize that Caterfly was no longer following her. Concerned, she turned around and retraced her flight through the garden. After a moment, she spotted Caterfly below. He was calmly munching a rose petal.

She fluttered down beside him and gave him a concerned look. She suspected he had crash landed and was happy to see that he didn't seem injured. Caterfly smiled warmly at her and offered her the rose petal. She enjoyed the savory treat and offered a smile in return for the present. After she finished eating, Caterfly surprised her by running ahead arching his back, turning his wings and leaving the ground.

At first, Peggy followed him through his awkward flight through the garden. She noticed he had difficulty in banking and turning. She maneuvered into a position just ahead of his right wing. He watched her closely and tried to duplicate her turning procedures. After many awkward attempts, he began laughing at himself. When Peggy heard his laughter, she began to laugh joyfully.

Many creatures of the garden floor looked upward to observe the spectacle above. Two insects were flying crazily above them; unreasonable laughter filled the air.

After a few more spectacular crashes, a weary Caterfly noticed it was noon. He decided to begin the landing procedure that Peggy taught him. He slowed the beat of his wings, he slowly lowered his head and watched the ground drift toward him on a moderate flight angle. Just as he was inches from the ground and a safe landing, a small gust of wind that was running along the ground flipped him tail over head on the soft grass floor of the garden. As he awkwardly rolled about trying to get his footing, Caterfly was joined by a giggling Peggy.

He motioned to her to look at the sun. She knew it was noon and nodded in agreement.

She broke the silence. "For you, that was a beautiful landing, Caterfly!" she said joyfully.

"Yes," he said smilingly. "Considering I couldn't

even fly an inch yesterday, Peggy. You must be brilliant! I can't imagine how you were able to get me flying."

"It was easy, Caterfly, once you believed you could and once you were willing to risk leaving the security of the ground. You fly awkwardly, but after a little experience, you will fly more gracefully. Later you will be able to get around using less and less energy to do so. Once you learn to conserve your strength while flying, you'll be able to extend your flight time without really tiring. Creatures like us don't fly very fast or very high, but we manage to get where we want to go."

"You are a great teacher, Peggy," he said. "The day I spend with you was the most enjoyable one I ever had."

"Why did you turn away from me last night?" she asked him in a more serious tone.

"I turned toward the light in the East," he said. "You were asleep and I didn't want to wake you to explain what I was doing."

"Why were you so fascinated by the light, Caterfly?"

"Because it grows more fascinating as I pursue it and open my mind to it. You must see the light; you must know what I'm talking about."

Peggy was silent for a moment before she answered. "All creatures see the light to some degree, Caterfly. Some feel that they are too far away to follow after it, some get caught up in their business and think they don't have time to follow it. Others see it so dimly that it doesn't influence them very much or attract them very strongly. I look at it as just one more thing that can't be explained, and I don't trouble myself thinking too much about it. Philosophers who think like you go over to religion. Maybe you'll end up there too."

She looked at him intently when she finished speaking.

Caterfly remained still.

Peggy spoke again. Softness and sweetness filled her voice.

"Caterfly, I want to be frank with you." She looked into his face as she spoke. "I could fall in love with you. I could love you, but I'm afraid to let it happen."

Caterfly did not speak. A moment passed.

"Caterfly," she said softly, "my life is my philosophy, my philosophy is my life. Without the pursuit of my ideals, I would grow unhappy and soon die. I must remain with the philosophers and gather all the support I can for my views. If you would stand by me from attacks on my ideas and help me win supporters, I would be very happy the rest of my days. Could you bring yourself to believe what I believe? Would you like to spend more and more of your time with me? What a pair we could make!"

Caterfly waited a moment and looked sincerely and meekly at his companion.

"I'll be frank with you too, Peggy, I can't begin to tell you what you already mean to me. You are the most lovely and the most brilliant creature I've met in my short life and long travels. This past day with you has been the most wonderful day in my life. Since I've met you, I've felt all kinds of new feelings. I believe in myself now; I see all kinds of new possibilities in my life—in life itself. You helped make all this possible."

"I'm most grateful," he continued, "That you spent a day of your precious life to make an awkward and difficult creature like me happy. The word difficult seems to sum me up. You told me to get the word 'can't' out of my life. Once I began to believe I could fly, I did fly. Don't you see, Peggy? The word 'can't' is in your philosophy. You say we *can't* learn about the world; I believe we can. You say the finite mind *can't* comprehend the infinite or the eternal. I'm not ready to say 'can't' on that one either.

I need time to finish my journey, time to find the answers I seek. I know what I am now, but I want to know what I will become. Once I learn what I'm becoming, I'll probably realize my purpose in life. Who knows, maybe I'll discover that you're right after all about everything."

Peggy tried not to show disappointment as she said to him, "Caterfly, what will you do now? Where will you go now?"

"I'm not sure, Peggy, but please understand I really don't want to leave you—not even for a moment. Wherever I go, I'll carry you in my heart. You see, I'm falling in love with you, Peggy. The trouble is I want to fall in love with you and find happiness at your side, and if I don't leave you soon, I won't have the strength to complete my journey."

Peggy eyed him warmly. "Is that such a bad fate, Caterfly?" she said as she anticipated his reply.

"Sooner or later the same questions that have driven me all of my life would begin to bother me and make me miserable if I didn't pursue their answers with the last ounce of my strength," he said in a very determined voice.

"I understand," she said. "I understand only too well. It would be selfish of me to try to hold on to you in your present state of mind. I believe you are sincere in what you say to me. We'll let some time pass and we'll see what happens. Please come back to me some day and tell me how you feel . . . about things. I know how to get on in this world. Just come to me someday and tell me what your adventure has brought. Maybe we could work something out."

Caterfly didn't answer. He looked deeply into the sincerity of her eyes and watched the tears form.

"What a fool I am," he thought. "How can I leave

her . . . for what? She's my life's mate. I'll never find another. She's filled with loveliness and brilliance. I'm happy in her presence. How can any force that drives me away from her be a good force. Why, oh why must I go?"

"Peggy," he said softly, "I care so much for you I find it painful to linger here. I must leave soon."

She nodded her head slowly in agreement. Her face was moist from tears.

"Peggy, I feel that I am coming to the end of my life's search. I will return to you someday soon if life affords me that joy. If I perish in my search, my last thought will be a thought of you. If I suffer, I'll think of you for consolation. I'll think of you and the friendly light—the light that has always led me. Somehow we're all involved in life together—you, me, the light, the gardens, the stars, the moon, the world with all its creatures."

In her sadness she hardly heard anything except his words on how he would think of her.

"I challenge you to do something, Caterfly," she said with as much firmness as she could muster in her voice.

"I like challenges," he said as he tried to overcome the wavering quality in his tone of voice.

"Without asking why, or without hesitating . . . or without looking back . . . when I turn away from you . . . I challenge you to fly away from me."

"It can't happen this fast," he thought. "Maybe this is the best way, though."

She turned her head away from his and closed her eyes.

Caterfly stroked Peggy's head once with his right wing and turned away from her. After an awkward running start, he leaped into the warm noon air. A flutter of tiny wings lifted him above the clumps of nearby grass.

Chapter 12

. . . in which Caterfly reaches the light.

As Caterfly fluttered awkwardly away from Peggy, his insect heart was filled with sorrow and doubt.

"Maybe there is no answer," he thought. "Maybe I'm crazy for leaving Peggy. Just meeting her has justified my entire trip. What will happen if I lose her? She has been so kind and helpful to me. She is so beautiful and wonderful."

He thus occupied himself until he approached the camp of religion. He flew over the area to get his bearings; he flew low to afford himself the best view. Caterfly quickly became startled and upset by the view below. The main area of the camp was divided into eight clearly defined sections. The sections, although different in size, had one thing in common—harsh looking walls. The dividing walls completely separated one religious group from the next. The walls themselves were constructed of stones, sticks, mud, and various types of thorns which stuck out in all directions.

Except for one species of large green beetle which inhabited one of the units, all of the other enclosed areas contained many species of insects, birds, and small rodents. Some of the religious groups were very quiet and remained in their quarters; others ran to and fro from their habitations and shouted into the narrow doorways of the enclosures of their neighbors.

During his overflight, Caterfly also noticed that in three of the enclosures below the participants were occupied in moving strangely colored stones and upright twigs about in a mysterious ceremony. By the time he ended his flight and perched on a large rose which overlooked the scene, the shock of the confusing sight wore off.

"They seem to be as mixed up and unhappy as most of the philosophers I observed," he thought. "Is there no way to find peace in this world? Does peace and happiness exist anywhere, or am I just a fool chasing an illusion? What makes me feel that I can find happiness when so many others have failed? Maybe I should go back to Peggy. Maybe she could be my purpose for living, but then again, I came this far; I might as well spend at least a day here. Who knows, the creatures here might be happy inside even though they look miserable and mean on the outside."

Caterfly was preparing to fly down to the north end of the camp when a sharp voice shattered the air.

"Infidel, how dare you profane God's holy rose with your sinful body. Depart immediately or you'll die for your transgression!"

Caterfly looked below his white rose platform and spied a huge green caterpillar making his way up the stem of the rose. The caterpillar bore such a menacing expression that Caterfly didn't hesitate a moment to argue with the defender of the roses.

As he fluttered groundward, he observed that most of the roses on the surrounding bushes were inhabited by the same type of caterpillar as the one who shouted at him. The caterpillars hummed messages to one another from their flower towers.

"I guess everything has its place except me," he thought as he landed on the north end of the camp of the religious.

Caterfly scurried toward the first enclosure which seemed small compared to the rest. Like all the others, it was almost entirely closed as it was surrounded by a menacing thorn-jutting wall. He was about to look in the narrow doorway when the old face of a Caddis-fly popped out, its eyes glaring at him. The Caddis-fly began shouting at him.

"Quickly, stranger, enter quickly. The world will soon come to an end! Save yourself! Join us!"

Caterfly remained silent.

The Caddis-fly shouted even louder, "Don't number yourself among the dammed who will be punished by demons forever in the underground. Join us. We are the elect. Join us! Leave that sinful world of ugliness and sorrow and prepare for the end with us. Quickly! Quickly!"

Caterfly moved away from the Caddis-fly and the elect and tried to clear his head. He crawled more slowly to the next habitation which was even smaller and poked his head inside. His inquisitive head was immediately rapped sharply by the bill of a hummingbird.

The fierce bird snarled at the stunned blue and white striped insect.

"Away sinner, only the elect dwell here!"

Caterfly quickly backed out of the doorway. He was angry and wanted to fight. His head hurt from what he thought was an unwarranted blow. He impulsively wanted to charge in and tangle with the hummingbird, but he checked his anger.

"I'll probably get killed in there," he thought.

After he calmed himself, he crawled to a much larger enclosure.

"I'm glad the hummingbird has found his salvation at least," he mumbled as he saw humor in the situation. "I just wonder why the elect and the elect don't get together and become one big elect."

He was surprised when he actually entered the third doorway without resistance. Although this enclosure seemed threatening on the outside, it was quite beautiful on the inside. All types of beautiful stones and colorful flower petals were positioned in strange but lovely patterns. Far back in the enclosure he noticed some activity. Some of the creatures were laborers; a few seemed to be administrators and a very small number were obviously teachers of religion. The workers hustled to and from the enclosure bringing food stuffs to the rest of the community, while the administrators directed them. The religion teachers seemed content in maintaining the beauty of the interior and advising the others on matters of proper conduct.

Caterfly became so engrossed in observing their activities that he did not see the giant orange snail approach him.

"Yes, my young visitor might I serve you?" the sweet voice of the snail broke his concentration.

Caterfly relaxed, he was disarmed by the easy manner of the giant snail. He faced the snail and spoke with deep sincerity ringing in his voice.

"My name is Caterfly. I've travelled a long way to find myself and my purpose in life. I've tried just about everything, and I've been disappointed by just about everything. From what I've seen of religion, it's all very confusing. Nothing I've seen around here from the air or on the ground makes much sense. I would like to hear your ideas on the subject."

The snail's eyes were filled with love as he spoke to Caterfly.

"My name is Henry, Caterfly. I belong to this religious community because I am happy here. I, like you and many others in the land of religion, travelled far to find myself and my purpose in life. I found what I was look‌ing for here—God."

"God?" Caterfly repeated.

"Yes, God," the giant orange snail repeated reverently.

"I heard the word once before," Caterfly said. "What does it mean?"

"I realize that most crea‌tures of the world don't know God, Caterfly, but you 'll know him if you don't already because you're a spiritual adventurer. God means all good. God created the world. God is all powerful. God loves all of us. Most of us will spend all eternity with God when we die. Our lives, unworthy as they are, should be spent seeking God and serving Him. Those of us who are in religion are supposed to be trying a little harder than the average creature to find and serve God."

"Henry," Caterfly responded, "does the service of God mean that creatures act cruelly to one another in any way? The reason I ask you this is because I don't see any justification for unkindness among creatures for any reason at all. Society, religion, philosophy have no jus‌tification to encourage unkindness," Caterfly said in a firm voice.

"I agree with you, Caterfly, but sometimes groups get so caught up in their zeal to find God and serve Him that they concentrate more on their differences from other groups than on their likenesses. My own group is guilty of this at times."

Caterfly smiled. He was pleased with Henry's hones‌ty.

"Tell me more about your group, Henry," he said.

"Like all religions, we believe in the basic goodness of all creatures. We believe that the spirit of all creatures is immortal. The spirit of those who love God will join God forever in heaven after death. The departed spirits of those who reject God will be tormented by the demons below forever. Our purpose in life is to learn to know God and love Him through service to others."

As the great snail spoke and the normal activity in the compound continued, questions were forming in Caterfly's insect brain.

"Henry, why would anyone reject a loving God?" he asked.

"The demons confuse creatures, they play tricks on us to lure us away from the goodness of God. Religion shows us what to do to stay on the path to reach Him. Each religion has its own rules to find God."

"Where did the rules come from, Henry?" Caterfly asked.

"God gave the correct rules to us a long time ago."

"God gave them to your group only?" Caterfly asked.

"Yes, God gave the true rules to our group only, the other groups think they have the rules, but they are ignorant of the truth," he answered confidently.

Henry's confidence only seemed to create more doubts in Caterfly's mind.

"If I tried to follow the rules of your religion, what would happen to me?"

"You would grow stronger and stronger in your faith of God, Caterfly. You would become the best possible you. You would serve others better and see God at the end of your life. Your destiny would be to live forever in happiness with God," the great snail said wh confidence ringing in his voice.

"You must forgive me, Henry, but I'm a difficult creature. Forgive me for saying so, because maybe I'm numbered among the dammed, but I have serious doubts about your religion or any organization like yours."

"Go ahead, speak out, Caterfly," the giant snail said in an understanding voice.

"I see great beauty in your religion, but I don't believe any creature will become any better or be saved by following any rules. We develop a habit of following rules by following rules, no much else. I feel a creature must first experience the truth and goodness of God, then all the rules of good conduct will be easy and natural for him to follow. The experience of God in itself, here and now, will charm any one of us to go in fast pursuit of Him all the rest of our days. The experience of the goodness of God will overpower the distracting power of the demons you spoke about. You might think my belief is wild or crazy, but it seems so real to me that I can't accept anything else."

For a long moment, Henry remained silent. He didn't seem at all surprised by Caterfly's views on religion.

Ironically, Caterfly was the surprised one. He was surprised by the words which flowed from him. He now realized that his thoughts had been secretly taking a definite form as he travelled toward his goal of truth. He was also surprised that his companion wasn't startled by what he thought was a very unique view on life and religion.

The giant snail smiled warmly at him and spoke in a kindly voice.

"Caterfly, you are indeed a spiritual adventurer. Your adventure has reached a danger point. Your pride and self-confidence in your views are blind. The laws of religions have survived in this vicious and changing world for millions of days. Creatures close to God have kept their integrity from change and attack. Who are you or who is any creature, for that matter, to demand to possess all happiness and eternal joy right now? You are young, Caterfly. As you grow older, you'll grow resigned to the long process of knowing God and being elevated by the Creator's graces. We all grow impatient at times, but we mustn't confuse our impatience to find God with the true way of finding Him—the way of the rules and constant struggling against evil distractions that lure us away from the true path. False pride is the worst distraction. Whenever I have thoughts like yours, I review the rules of my faith and try to forget the annoying thoughts. The more I study the rules of faith, the more I believe in them and the less I am distracted by the kind of thoughts that now obsess you."

Caterfly listened respectfully as his well-meaning companion spoke to him.

"Henry, maybe you're right, but I feel so right about my views that I must pursue them with all my strength until I experience the full joy of God while I live—or die trying."

"I feel that you are on a very dangerous adventure, Caterfly, but I can give you one consolation," the orange snail said after some reflection. "From what I've been able to learn over the many days I've lived, certain rare creatures in various religions have claimed to have had the experience you're seeking. My superior told me that many, many days ago, a worm lived here who was filled with joy and happiness. He bubbled over with kindness and wisdom. My superior said that he heard the worm got that way by perfectly following our rules. No one knows for certain. Perhaps he was given a special blessing from God. The question is, does God also bless the mystics, as we call them, of other religions as well? Be careful, Caterfly! You're trying to force your way into absolute happiness. You can't force God. Stay with us, follow our rules. You will have an eternity to discover the full joy of God after your body dies. Who knows, after many days of faithfully following the rules of our faith, God might grant you the joy of the mystics."

"Thank you for your concern and kindness, Henry," Caterfly said. "I wish it were only pride driving me; my life would have been much easier. I am haunted by a truth that grows stronger everyday. Goodbye, Henry. I would like to stay with you and accept everything you say, but I must continue to search and find out for myself." Caterfly began to turn away from his companion.

Henry also gave his farewell, "Goodbye, Caterfly, may the light of God guide you in your journey."

The word "light" stopped Caterfly in his tracks. He turned and faced Henry.

"Henry, what do you mean by light?"

Henry was surprised by Caterfly's unexpected question.

"Why, that's the way we say goodbye to our friends here. We've been taught that God is the God of light as well as the God of truth. The light of God guides all creatures. Miserable creatures as we are, we never see the light too brightly in this life, but heaven is filled with the light of God."

Caterfly stared at Henry for a long moment and took another look at the interior of the religious compound.

"I could almost be happy here," he thought, "but the light itself attracts me more strongly than any resting place. When I solve the mystery of the light, I'll solve the mystery of myself. When I discover who I am and what my purpose is, I'll be happy anywhere."

Henry's mention of the "light" generated fresh hope and courage in the blue and white striped insect, but the words "demons" and "pride" stuck in his head and jammed his thoughts as he crawled slowly away from the enclosure.

"Such harsh concepts," he thought. "I wonder if the demons that drive us to distraction are only instincts we don't understand. I wonder if my desire to find myself is just a bigger demon than all the rest of my other demons. Is my pursuit of the light just the folly of blind pride?" His thoughts troubled him, but he kept moving.

He spent the remainder of his first day at the religious camp attempting conversations with many participants of the religious communities. Some spoke to him kindly, others used terminology he couldn't understand, some shouted at him, others dammed him to a life with the demons, and a mosquito went as far as to call him a demon. As night fell, he crawled eastward through the area and approached the bright center of the ever blossoming, ever radiant light which seemed closer than ever. The whole world seemed to be covered with the lovely radiance.

When Caterfly stole a backward glance, he thought sadly, "If only the religionists would break down their walls and open their hearts to one another, the light would engulf them all!"

Caterfly marched steadily onward. Tears filled both of his eyes as the world around him filled more and more abundantly with the soft radiant light. His pace slowed; he could see nothing except the light. His whole being filled with joy.

"I'm here at last!" he thought joyfully. "I'm actually here at last!"

He noticed a little movement in a vague form on his right.

"Another creature has found the light!" he thought happily.

He edged toward a small creature about half his size. His companion in the light was so absorbed in its charming glow that he didn't seem to notice Caterfly. As Caterfly closed the gap between them he saw that the small creature was a brown bee with a youthful face.

"How joyful he looks," thought Caterfly. "Does he live here, I wonder? Is he a mystic or what? He seems to enjoy the light even more than I do. What does all this mean?"

Caterfly remained by the side of the brown bee throughout the night. At times, the light seemed to come in waves. At times, the light seemed to wax and wane in its brilliance.

Caterfly felt great peace bathing himself in the soothing, charming light.

"I wish Peggy were here," he thought as he drifted away in peaceful slumber.

Chapter 13

. . .in which he discovers brother-hood among many different crea-tures.

When morning came, Caterfly found himself sur-rounded by a dozen serene looking creatures of various types.

"Welcome, Caterfly," a brown water scorpion happily greeted him.

"Why, hello!" he said in a startled voice.

"How do you know my name?"

"Our little master told us your name," answered a shiny black weevil.

"He asked us to attend to a new arrival, Caterfly, the brave adventurer who will stop at nothing short of peace and truth," the water scorpion added.

Caterfly was about to ask his new companions how their little master knew his name, but a large wolf spider asked him a question before he could form his words.

"Are you here to learn from the little master?" the wolf spider inquired.

Caterfly observed the happy lot of creatures and answered, "I don't know. It depends upon what he is teaching."

"How will you know what he is teaching until you

become his student!" a grey sparrow challenged with laughter in his voice.

Caterfly too found himself laughing along with the good natured group.

"Is this the journey's end?" Caterfly thought. "Will I find my answers and my peace here with this happy band?"

"We are going now to listen to the little master," the wolf spider said cheerfully. "Would you like to join us?"

"I know you mean well by asking me, but if your little master says one thing in favor of war or anything to justify any type of unkindness among creatures or anything to narrow down a creature's hopes or frustrate an honest quest for answers about the universe, I will leave immediately! I am telling you this because I don't want you to be disappointed if you see me scurrying away in the middle of the lecture."

Caterfly paused. The group was silent.

"You see, I'm a difficult creature, maybe a selfish one, too. If your teacher can show me how to find peace and happiness without rules that close out others and help me to help my fellow creatures if they need it— regardless of their instincts and life styles—then I will listen carefully to his every word.

"If he helps me to find myself and accept myself for what I am, then I will follow him forever; your little teacher would then become my little teacher."

"Bravo, bravo, Caterfly!" the little band of seekers cheered emphatically.

Caterfly was surprised by their reaction. He was about to apologize for stating his views so strongly, but they seemed overjoyed by his attitude.

"They seem to vibrate happiness," Caterfly thought. "They remind me of the participants I observed in that cheerful compound yesterday. They jumped up and down shouting the name of God as loud as they could. They seemed exhilarated during their ceremony, but they seemed less joyful after they settled down. These creatures seem exhilarated without the shouting or jumping. What are they doing to get this way? What does all this mean?" he thought as the band arrived at the scene of the lecture.

The little brown bee sat on the flower of a morning glory in a small open spot of ground surrounded by various wild flowering plants.

The group that accompanied Caterfly joined another smaller group that formed a semicircle around the small brown bee.

The entire group fell immediately silent. Caterfly felt an ocean of peace and joy emanating from the little brown bee. The audience seemed intent on hearing every word uttered by the teacher.

While the teacher paused a moment, Caterfly edged through the throng to be close to the brown bee. He climbed the stem of a small plant and sat on the leaf nearest the bee. He looked quite ordinary to Caterfly except for his joyful expression and his extraordinarily beautiful eyes.

Caterfly was spellbound. "Such happiness in those eyes," he thought. "He doesn't have to talk. I could sit here all day and get inspiration just by looking at him."

The brown bee turned to him and smiled. The bee's expression seemed to be saying, "Welcome, Caterfly, it's about time you found us."

"What is happening here?" Caterfly thought.

The little teacher began to talk to his students. His voice was filled with energy, strength, but yet sweetness and softness.

"We are very fortunate to share such a lovely sunny day. We must remember that the sun always shines even though we may not see it at times. The light of truth, the joy of the universe awaits us if we are but willing to take the simple, but necessary steps to attain all the goodness and joy in the cosmos.

"This is our natural state; the only state of mind and heart that makes us enduringly happy—the state of being one with the truth and love and fills the universe—the state of mind that makes us one with the loving Creator of the worlds and all the creatures of the worlds. This is the natural state of all creatures, but most creatures do not believe big enough to leave their smallness for the grandness of their highest selves, the Self Himself, the Creator.

"Most creatures turn all their attention to the outside world. They turn outward for the purpose of survival and enjoyment, but the fuller, richer joy of their highest self is to be found within."

The teacher paused for a moment to give his students time to digest what he was saying.

"Yes, yes!" Caterfly thought, "but please don't tell us to fence off others or kill them to find our own happiness." He continued to think hopefully.

The teacher continued.

"We can't tell the creatures of this world to forget about their survival in their environment or their enjoyment of their environment. That obviously is not the answer. We cannot tell them to abandon their life styles and simply live within themselves. They would not listen. They would be right for not listening. We also cannot tell creatures to throw away their existing beliefs, since beliefs usually indicate a state in the development of the experiences and psychology of an individual creature. We might try to show an average creature a highly complicated system for drawing nearer to his highest self, but he won't be able to comprehend it or master it in the short space of his lifetime."

The teacher paused again.

Caterfly's thoughts grew troubled. "This is the point where all philosophies and religions seem to stop. The question is whether or not it is possible for a creature to go on the ultimate adventure and explore God Himself. Is it possible for a creature to find all peace, all truth, and all joy in his short lifetime? Is a tiny creature just limited to his tiny mind and heart forever, or can he go beyond all his limitations and find his highest self, his highest joy in his tiny life span?"

The teachers's voice once again pleasantly broke the silence of the attentive assemblage.

"There is a simple method we can offer to others, anyone can easily learn to use it. Any creature of any set of beliefs can enjoy this method. It is an innocent procedure, since it causes only good to the user; it offers no obstacle to anyone's religion or philosophy. This simple procedure will lead the mind of the practitioner inward, since the mind is charmed by a greater and greater experience of the highest self. The mind after a little while is drawn ever and ever closer to the Absolute Being. This charming experience is very easy and natural. There is no resistance involved or discipline required. We call this method deep meditation for lack of a better name. The practitioner of our meditation technique finds himself growing happier and happier each day he dives inward. His conscious awareness grows as tensions within him break up and he perceives the essential harmony in the universe. The truth or falsehood of his own beliefs become clear to him; the light within him becomes so bright that evil and error no longer have sway over him.

"In this way he functions better in his environment. He lives a full rich life within and without. After awhile, he experiences pure consciousness. As he continues in meditation, he will experience Cosmic Consciousness and unity with God Himself. God is love and as love He draws us to Himself for what better fate could He give us?

"The natural state of our heart and mind is unity with the highest self. All the powers within us will take us there if we but give them a chance. Deep meditation is such a chance; a chance for all of us to return to the source of all good, all truth, all joy, all light."

Caterfly was spellbound. His tiny mind was racing wildly.

"Yes, yes, yes!" he thought joyfully. "There must be a

way around all obstacles of the understanding. There must be a way of finding all joy right now! This is not the end of my journey, it is the beginning of new hope!"

"Teacher, I can accept what you say," a large grey roach addressed the brown bee, "but can we make others believe?"

"Yes, from our own lives, for one thing," the brown bee answered. "If other creatures see a natural joy flowing from us, they will be attracted to find the cause of it. When we explain the cause, some will try our meditation and others will be drawn away by the fascination of the world.

"We will teach this meditation to all who want to learn it. Those who try it will bring many others to us."

"Teacher!" a bright green toad called out, "why are we just hearing about this method now? After all, the gardens and the creatures of the gardens have been around for a long time. Other philosophies and religions have been around since ancient times."

"The method that I speak about is ancient. In some places in ancient times, it was very popular. Despite its effectiveness, the knowledge of it was corrupted in inept politicians and those who fear it threatened their control over various religious groups. We believe that a few of the founders of the great religions practiced this form of meditation and passed the knowledge on to their followers who lost the practice in its pure form as thousands of years passed. With your help, it will once again become a popular method to find the Absolute."

"Little master, is this the only way to find God in a short space of time?" a speckled fly asked him.

"Almost all religions lead to God," the little brown bee answered. "Most creatures who carefully follow the rules of their religion have some experience of the truth and goodness of God in their lifetimes. Very few except those who are regarded as mystics arrive at the full oneness of Absolute light, love, and joy in their lifetimes.

"Deep meditation, if faithfully practiced, will quickly evolve a creature's consciousness and heart into that most glorious union with his Creator. Most societies and religions have essentially sound rules which help produce safety and productivity in the community. There is no struggle in the individual to come up to the best standards of religion and society once his consciousness and heart are in unity with the Absolute. Deeper and deeper experiences of the joy within make all of life seem easier."

"Are there any more questions today?" the brown bee said warmly, his eyes all aglow.

Caterfly had many questions, but he felt they would be out of place in the general assembly. He watched the brown bee descend from his seat on the morning glory and disappear through the crowd of joyful students.

Caterfly's mind was still whirling with questions as the throng of joyful students also disappeared from the scene.

"Every word he said had the ring of truth to it," he thought. "How can I learn this meditation? Will it really work for me? How long will it take to work? Would I have to remain here once I learned it? How deeply could I dive inward, since I'm such a small insect?"

"Caterfly," a voice called to him from nearby.

Caterfly turned to see his acquaintance, the shiny black weevil waiting for him under a white rose bush.

"Caterfly, would you like to learn to meditate?" the weevil asked him as he approached the smiling black bug.

"You know I would!" Caterfly responded emphatically.

"Come with me, Caterfly, and I will teach you a little about the method each day for three days. On the fourth day, if your desire to meditate is unchanged, I'll give you your mantra," the weevil said to Caterfly as they crawled along together.

"What is a mantra?" Caterfly asked as if it were some strange disease.

"Don't worry, you'll see, Caterfly. You'll see," the black bug said.

Chapter 14

. . . *in which Caterfly reaches his goal and ends his journey.*

"You are about to undertake the greatest of all journeys, the journey inward," the black weevil spoke calmly to Caterfly. Three days had passed. Caterfly had made his decision to be initiated into meditation.

"The mantra that I will give you is simply a vehicle to draw your mind inward to the ever increasing joy and charm of your highest self. There is no magic to it; no real concentration is needed."

Caterfly listened intently.

"Remember, Caterfly, my instructions on using the mantra. Don't anticipate too much. Generally, the mantra works in subtle ways on the consciousness, refining it little by little. Persistent use of the mantra over a period of time will bring all the benefits our teacher speaks about. Many others have successfully taken the journey. No matter what happens next, meditate faithfully each sunset and each sunrise. Are you ready?"

"Yes, I'm ready," Caterfly responded. "I'm ready."

"Good, listen to your mantra. Repeat it after me to get used to it then never repeat it aloud again. In the future, when you meditate first gently think it the way I instructed you to use it. Now, please repeat your mantra after me."

Caterfly felt the warmth of the bright sunrise and smelled the delicious fragrance of the rose bushes around him and relaxed. His young teacher uttered the mantra to him. Caterfly repeated the strange sounding word to his teacher. The teacher again uttered the word, but more softly. Caterfly again repeated the word but softly. The teacher then pronounced the word almost inaudibly. The blue and white striped insect did the same.

The teacher was silent.

Caterfly repeated the word mentally; the journey had begun. The teacher smiled, but Caterfly could not see him through his gently closed eyes.

Caterfly continued to repeat the mantra gently; joy and peace flooded the heart of the blue and white striped insect; the light within him grew brighter and brighter.

Caterfly continued the inward journey by repeating the word. Tears poured out of his closed eyes as joy filled every fiber of his being. A feeling of unity and happiness grew within him as wave after wave of life enriching light and joy ebbed gently into his consciousness. Finite dimensions faded away into infinite formlessness.

He lost track of time and place; he even forgot who he was and what he was doing as the mantra seemed to repeat itself and charm his mind and heart toward greater and deeper regions of joy within.

He became both participant and spectator of the glorious journey; deep within his being he heard his own awe filled voice sobbing, "Yes, yes, oh yes," A nudge from his companion told him it was time for him to begin to come out of his meditation.

He slowly began to open his eyes. Everything seemed to take on a subtle softness, a lovely radiance, as he began to look about.

"Take your time coming out," the weevil whispered.

Caterfly smiled joyfully at the shiny black weevil.

"You were fortunate since your first dive inward was very, very deep. You will have days, understand, when your meditation seems to go nowhere. It will be working just the same. If you remember at that time that it is simply working on a less obvious level, you'll never get discouraged. Just keep meditating and everything will be fine. Balance meditation and activity for a full rich life."

Caterfly's eyes were still moist as he spoke to the initiator. "You gave me something to help me to find the light, joy, and truth that I've sought all of my days. I still have unanswered questions about myself or I should say my smaller self, but the ever expanding joy and charm of my higher self will gradually satisfy all my questions, I'm sure."

The weevil nodded his head in agreement.

"I feel the greatest purpose I can have in this world is to do what you are doing to give others a chance to find joy and light within themselves. This is the work I'd like to do in the world. I admire the creatures of the gardens and their participation in life's challenges. I could learn a lot from them, and maybe some of them could learn something meaningful from me."

"You have been a brave adventurer and an excellent student, Caterfly; I do hope you join us. We need you. Please see the little master and tell him how you feel. I'm sure he'll wish to give you the special training necessary to impart mantras to all those who are interested in diving inward."

Caterfly gratefully hugged his instructor and flew as quickly as he could through an open space in the rose plants toward a gently sloping grassy knoll. The tiny brown bee was sitting on the knoll enjoying the sights and sounds of the day.

As Caterfly landed awkwardly by his side, his energetic but sweet voice greeted the blue and white striped insect. "Hello, Caterfly, I hope you are enjoying this lovely day."

"Hello, little master," Caterfly responded as he edged closer to more fully enjoy the effects of the brown bee's joyful eyes.

"You know why I'm here, don't you?" Caterfly said to him with deep respect and sincerity in his voice.

"Yes, Caterfly, I do. Once the fort of cosmic consciousness is captured, all obstacles to the understanding become child's play. Continue to meditate and you will know what I mean. It is a custom that the student ask the teacher for acceptance in his own words, however," the tiny brown bee said with a twinkle in his eye.

"Little Master, I am just Caterfly, a difficult and stubborn insect who crawls slowly, flies awkwardly, and has had a difficult time settling down. Despite these problems, I am grateful just to exist in any form in God's garden because He is all joy, all light, and all truth. I am happy just to exist and to have the opportunity to come closer to Him and His creatures each day.

"I am also grateful to have learned a way to find my highest self more quickly. I would like to dedicate my short life to bring this knowledge to others, regardless of their philosophies, religions, or life styles. Everyone could benefit from this. I can think of no better way to spend my life."

"Well spoken, gentle Caterfly!" the little bee chuckled.

"I'm just a little brown bee who also flies awkwardly. My body is too big for my wings, they say. I'm just what you say, a little master. I'm master of no one except myself. My ambition for mastery does not go beyond that. I'm a little master and a little teacher, but great master and great teachers will pass through these gardens someday just as they passed through in ancient times.

"As tiny as we are, we have infinite potential for helping others recognize the truth of the great masters and teachers when they hear it in the wind or stumble upon it in the ground.

"Yes, I will teach you how to impart the technique to all others who seek it. I am grateful to have you as a student; I hope to prove to be a good teacher."

Caterfly's eyes were moist again. He looked deeply into the eyes of his teacher. Neither insect spoke.

"I'm accepted!" Caterfly thought. "This is just the beginning of a new journey! Does he know how I long to see Peggy again. Does he know how anxious I am to see if Peggy will try this meditation? Can he possibly know how much I want Peggy to be my life long partner in helping others? Is he aware of how much I want to talk to Harry, Homer, Esmeralda, Black Jack, Henry, Bos, and Mr. Frog about my discoveries?"

He looked deeper into the eyes of his teacher.

The eyes of the little brown bee twinkled joyfully.

QUEST BOOKS

are published by
The Theosophical Society in America,
a branch of a world organization
dedicated to the promotion of brotherhood and
the encouragement of the study of religion,
philosophy, and science, to the end that man may
better understand himself and his place in
the universe. The Society stands for complete
freedom of individual search and belief.
In the Theosophical Classics Series
well-known occult works are made
available in popular editions.

CATERFLY is a QUEST book

published by
The Theosophical Publishing House
306 West Geneva Road
Wheaton, Illinois 60187

Write for a complete catalog of our books on
Asian classics, astrology, healing, occultism and
mysticism, philosophy, psychology, reincarnation,
religion, theosophy, yoga and meditation.